Forex Trading:

*Decoding the Secrets of the Forex Market for Consistent
Profits, Financial Freedom, and Success with Expert
Navigation Techniques*

Lewis Finan

Table of Contents

Introduction:

Welcome to the exciting world of Forex trading, where opportunities to achieve financial freedom and success await those who dare to venture into the dynamic and ever-evolving realm of foreign exchange.

In this book, "Forex Trading: Decoding the Secrets of the Forex Market for Consistent Profits, Financial Freedom, and Success with Expert Navigation Techniques," we embark on an insightful journey to unlock the mysteries of the Forex market and equip you with the knowledge and skills to navigate it with confidence and expertise.

The Forex market, also known as the foreign exchange or currency market, is the largest and most liquid financial market in the world. With trillions of dollars traded daily, it presents an unparalleled platform for individuals and institutions to engage in currency exchange and speculate on price movements. However, amidst its vast potential lies complexity, uncertainty, and the risk of substantial losses for the unprepared.

Our primary objective in this book is to unravel the enigmatic aspects of Forex trading and empower you with practical strategies, expert navigation techniques, and the mindset required to achieve consistent profits. Whether you are a seasoned trader seeking to enhance your skills or a novice with dreams of financial independence, this comprehensive guide is tailored to cater to your needs.

The Structure of the Book:

Understanding the Forex Market: We begin our journey by laying a solid foundation, acquainting you with the fundamental concepts, terminologies, and mechanisms that govern the Forex market. You will grasp the significance of currency pairs, exchange rates, and the factors influencing price movements.

The Art of Technical Analysis: Unleashing the power of charts and indicators, we delve into the art of technical analysis. You will learn to decipher historical price data and identify patterns, trends, and critical levels that can be exploited for profitable trades.

Mastering Fundamental Analysis: Beyond charts, fundamental analysis is the cornerstone of informed decision-making in Forex trading. We will explore how economic indicators, geopolitical events, and global macroeconomic trends shape currency movements.

Developing Your Trading Strategy: Building on the knowledge gained, we guide you through the process of formulating a personalized trading strategy that aligns with your risk appetite, goals, and preferences. We emphasize the importance of discipline, risk management, and adaptability.

The Psychology of a Successful Trader: Understanding your mind and emotions is pivotal in achieving consistent success. We shed light on the psychological challenges faced by traders and provide techniques to develop a resilient and focused trading mindset.

Advanced Techniques and Expert Insights: Elevating your trading prowess, we introduce you to advanced techniques employed by seasoned traders. Additionally, we offer expert insights and real-life experiences shared by successful professionals to inspire and guide you on your journey.

In closing, "Forex Trading: Decoding the Secrets of the Forex Market for Consistent Profits, Financial Freedom, and Success with Expert Navigation Techniques" endeavors to be your compass in the vast and often turbulent seas of Forex trading. We believe that armed with the knowledge, skills, and discipline acquired from this book, you will set sail towards consistent profits and unlock the gateway to financial independence.

Remember, success in Forex trading is not a secret to be uncovered, but rather a continuous journey of learning, adaptation, and growth. Let us embark together on this transformative voyage, and may your dreams of prosperity become a reality.

Understanding Forex Trading:

Forex trading, also known as foreign exchange trading or currency trading, is the process of buying and selling currencies in the global foreign exchange market. This decentralized and over-the-counter market enables participants, including individuals, banks, financial institutions, corporations, and governments, to exchange one currency for another at agreed-upon exchange rates.

Key Features of Forex Trading:

- Market Accessibility: The Forex market operates 24 hours a day, five days a week, making it one of the most accessible financial markets globally. Traders can engage in transactions at any time, as trading sessions overlap across different time zones.
- Liquidity: The Forex market is exceptionally liquid due to its immense size and the high volume of daily trading activities. This liquidity ensures that traders can buy or sell currencies quickly without significantly impacting exchange rates.
- Currency Pairs: Forex trading involves the exchange of currency pairs, where one currency is bought while another is sold simultaneously. Popular currency pairs include EUR/USD

(Euro/US Dollar), USD/JPY (US Dollar/Japanese Yen), and GBP/USD (British Pound/US Dollar).

- Bid and Ask Price: The bid price represents the highest price a buyer is willing to pay for a particular currency pair, while the asking price denotes the lowest price a seller is willing to accept. The difference between these two prices is known as the spread, which is how brokers make their profits.

- Leverage and Margin: Forex brokers often offer leverage, allowing traders to control larger positions in the market with only a fraction of the total trade value. However, high leverage also increases the risk of substantial losses, making risk management crucial.

- Factors Influencing Exchange Rates: Exchange rates are influenced by various factors, including economic indicators (e.g., GDP, inflation, employment), geopolitical events, interest rates, and market sentiment. Traders use fundamental and technical analysis to predict future price movements.

Trading Methods:

- Spot Market: In the spot market, currencies are bought and sold for immediate delivery at the prevailing market price. Transactions are settled within two business days, known as the "spot date."

- Forward Market: In the forward market, traders agree to exchange currencies at a predetermined price on a specific future date. This allows participants to hedge against potential currency fluctuations.

- Futures Market: Similar to forwards, currency futures involve contracts to buy or sell currencies at a fixed price on a specified date. However, futures are standardized and traded on organized exchanges.

- Options Market: Currency options grant traders the right, but not the obligation, to buy or sell currencies at a predetermined price on or before a specified date. This offers more flexibility compared to futures and forwards.

Risks and Rewards:

Forex trading offers the potential for significant profits, but it also carries inherent risks. Due to leverage, even small market movements can result in substantial gains or losses. Traders must approach the market with a well-defined strategy, risk management plan, and a disciplined mindset.

In conclusion, understanding Forex trading is essential for those looking to participate in this exciting and dynamic market. With proper education, analysis, and risk management, traders can navigate the Forex market with confidence, aiming for consistent profits while managing potential risks effectively.

The Importance of Expert Navigation Techniques:

Forex trading, with its vast potential for profits, can also be a challenging and complex endeavor. The ever-changing market dynamics, high volatility, and the presence of numerous participants make it essential for traders to develop and implement expert navigation techniques. These techniques, honed through experience and knowledge, play a crucial role in a trader's ability to achieve consistent profits and long-term success in the Forex market. Let's explore the significance of these expert navigation techniques:

1. Risk Management:

Expert navigation techniques emphasize the importance of effective risk management. Forex trading involves inherent risks, and a trader must protect their capital from significant losses. Implementing proper risk management techniques, such as setting stop-loss orders and position sizing, ensures that a trader can withstand market fluctuations without facing catastrophic consequences.

2. Technical Analysis Skills:

A proficient trader masters technical analysis, the study of historical price charts and patterns, to identify potential trading opportunities. Expert navigation techniques help traders interpret technical indicators, chart patterns, and support/resistance levels to make informed decisions based on price action.

3. Fundamental Analysis Insights:

Understanding fundamental analysis is essential in deciphering the macroeconomic factors that influence currency movements. Expert navigation techniques enable traders to interpret economic data, geopolitical events, central bank policies, and other fundamental factors to anticipate long-term trends.

4. Trading Strategy Development:

Having a well-defined trading strategy tailored to one's risk tolerance and trading style is crucial. Expert navigation techniques guide traders in developing robust strategies that adapt to changing market conditions, maximizing profit potential while minimizing risks.

5. Emotional Discipline:

Emotions can be a trader's greatest adversary. Expert navigation techniques focus on emotional discipline, teaching traders to manage fear, greed, and impulsiveness. Emotional stability enables traders to make rational decisions and stick to their trading plans even during challenging market conditions.

6. Timing and Patience:

Knowing when to enter and exit trades is critical for successful trading. Expert navigation techniques help traders identify favorable entry and exit points, as well as when to exercise patience and refrain from impulsive actions.

7. Continuous Learning and Adaptation:

The Forex market is dynamic and constantly evolving. Expert navigation techniques emphasize the importance of continuous learning and adaptation to stay ahead of market trends, new strategies, and technological advancements.

8. Capital Preservation:

Protecting and preserving capital is as important as making profits. Expert navigation techniques prioritize the preservation of capital, ensuring that a trader can continue participating in the market over the long term.

9. Market Analysis and Strategy Refinement:

Expert traders constantly analyze market data and refine their strategies. Through meticulous analysis and evaluation of past trades, they identify strengths and weaknesses, allowing them to optimize their approach to trading.

In the highly competitive and unpredictable world of Forex trading, expert navigation techniques play a pivotal role in achieving consistent profits and long-term success. By developing a comprehensive understanding of risk management, technical and fundamental analysis, emotional discipline, and continuous learning, traders can navigate the Forex market with confidence, resilience, and a higher probability of achieving their financial goals. These techniques form the foundation of a trader's journey toward becoming a skilled and profitable participant in the exciting world of Forex trading.

Chapter 1: The Basics of Forex Trading

Forex trading, short for foreign exchange trading, is a dynamic and lucrative financial market where currencies are bought and sold. It is the largest and most liquid financial market globally, with a daily trading volume exceeding $6 trillion. This chapter will serve as an introduction to the fundamentals of Forex trading, covering its history, market participants, currency pairs, and the mechanisms that drive price movements.

1. History of Forex Trading:

The concept of Forex trading dates back to ancient times when merchants engaged in currency exchange to facilitate international trade. However, modern Forex trading as we know it began to take shape in the 1970s when the Bretton Woods system, which fixed exchange rates to the US Dollar, collapsed. This led to the establishment of a free-floating exchange rate system, and global financial institutions started trading currencies to manage risks and speculate on exchange rate fluctuations.

2. Understanding the Forex Market:

The Forex market operates as an over-the-counter (OTC) market, meaning there is no centralized exchange. Instead, currency trading takes place electronically through a network of banks, brokers, financial institutions, and individual traders. The absence of a physical location and continuous trading hours (24/5) enable participants from all around the world to engage in trading.

3. Market Participants:

Several key players participate in the Forex market, each with distinct objectives:

- Banks and Financial Institutions: Major international banks conduct the largest portion of Forex trading, catering to corporate clients, institutions, and governments seeking foreign exchange services.
- Central Banks: Central banks intervene in the Forex market to stabilize their country's currency or implement monetary policies. Their actions can significantly impact exchange rates.
- Corporations: Multinational corporations engage in Forex trading to hedge against currency risks resulting from international business operations.
- Retail Traders: Individual traders, including retail investors, speculators, and hobbyists, access the Forex market through online platforms provided by brokers.

4. Currency Pairs:

In Forex trading, currencies are traded in pairs. The first currency in the pair is the base currency, and the second is the quote currency. The exchange rate represents the value of the quoted currency required to purchase one unit of the base currency. For example, in the EUR/USD currency pair, the Euro is the base currency, and the US Dollar is the quote currency. The exchange rate of EUR/USD at a given time might be 1.2000, meaning one Euro is worth 1.20 US Dollars.

5. Major Currency Pairs:

There are three categories of currency pairs in Forex trading: major, minor, and exotic. Major pairs consist of the most liquid and heavily traded currencies. These include EUR/USD, USD/JPY, GBP/USD, and USD/CHF. Major pairs are popular among traders due to their high liquidity and narrow spreads.

6. Minor and Exotic Currency Pairs:

Minor pairs involve the major currencies against other less commonly traded currencies. Examples include EUR/GBP, GBP/JPY, and AUD/NZD. Exotic pairs pair a major currency with a currency from an emerging or less developed economy. Exotic pairs might include USD/TRY (US Dollar/Turkish Lira) or EUR/TRY.

7. Forex Market Mechanics:

Forex trading involves two types of transactions: buying (going long) and selling (going short). When a trader believes that the value of the base currency will rise against the quoted currency, they go long. Conversely, when they believe the base currency will decline, they go short. The goal is to profit from price fluctuations.

8. Bid and Ask Price:

In Forex trading, each currency pair has two prices: the bid price and the asking price. The bid price represents the highest price a buyer is willing to pay for the currency pair, while the asking price is the lowest price a seller is willing to accept. The difference between the bid and ask price is known as the spread, which represents the broker's profit.

9. Leverage and Margin:

Leverage allows traders to control positions larger than their initial investment. It is expressed as a ratio, such as 1:100 or 1:500. For example, with 1:100 leverage, a $1000 margin can control a $100,000 position. While leverage magnifies potential profits, it also increases the risk of significant losses, making proper risk management essential.

10. Market Liquidity:

The Forex market's liquidity refers to the ease with which currencies can be bought or sold without significantly affecting prices. Major currency pairs are highly liquid due to their widespread use and the large number of participants. In contrast, exotic currency pairs tend to have lower liquidity and wider spreads.

11. Factors Affecting Forex Prices:

Forex prices are influenced by a wide range of factors, including:

- Economic Indicators: Economic data, such as GDP growth, inflation rates, employment figures, and retail sales, influence a country's currency strength.
- Interest Rates: Central banks' decisions on interest rates affect the value of their respective currencies. Higher interest rates typically attract foreign investment and strengthen the currency.
- Geopolitical Events: Political instability, trade disputes, and geopolitical tensions can cause currency fluctuations.
- Market Sentiment: Investor perceptions and market sentiment play a significant role in Forex price movements.

12. Trading Sessions:

The Forex market operates 24 hours a day, five days a week, with four major trading sessions: the Sydney session, the Tokyo session, the London session, and the New York session. These sessions overlap, creating periods of high trading activity and increased volatility.

13. Forex Trading Platforms:

To participate in Forex trading, traders use trading platforms provided by brokers. These platforms offer real-time price charts, technical indicators, and tools for executing trades.

14. Long-Term Investing vs. Short-Term Trading:

Forex trading accommodates both long-term investing and short-term trading strategies. Long-term investors focus on fundamental analysis and trends, holding positions for weeks, months, or even years. Short-term traders, on the other hand, rely on technical analysis and capitalize on intraday price movements.

15. The Role of Central Banks in Forex Trading:

Central banks' actions, such as interest rate decisions and currency interventions, have a significant impact on Forex prices. Traders must closely monitor central bank announcements and be prepared for sudden market shifts.

16. Understanding Pips:

Pip stands for "percentage in point" and is the smallest price movement that a currency pair can make. Most currency pairs are quoted to four or five decimal places, with one pip representing the last decimal place. For example, if the EUR/USD moves from 1.2000 to 1.2005, it has risen by five pips.

17. The Role of Brokers:

Forex brokers act as intermediaries, facilitating currency trades between buyers and sellers. They offer trading platforms, leverage, access to the market, and other services. It is essential for traders to choose a reputable and regulated broker to ensure fair and secure trading.

18. Market Orders and Pending Orders:

Traders can execute trades using market orders or pending orders. Market orders are executed at the current market price while pending orders are set to trigger when the market reaches a specified price level. Pending orders allow traders to plan and automate their entries and exits.

19. The Importance of Demo Trading:

Before risking real money, new traders should practice with demo accounts offered by brokers. Demo trading allows them to familiarize themselves with the trading platform, test strategies, and gain experience without financial risk.

This chapter has provided an essential foundation for understanding the basics of Forex trading. As a vast and intricate market, Forex trading offers immense potential for profit and personal growth. However, it is crucial for traders to continue their education, develop a sound trading strategy, and practice disciplined risk management to succeed in this exciting and dynamic arena. In the subsequent chapters of this book, we will delve deeper into advanced trading techniques, analysis methods, and strategies that will equip you with the necessary tools to navigate the Forex market with confidence and achieve consistent profits.

1.1 What is Forex?

Forex, short for foreign exchange, refers to the global financial market where currencies are traded. It is the largest and most liquid financial market in the world, facilitating the exchange of currencies between individuals, businesses, financial institutions, governments, and central banks. The Forex market operates 24 hours a day, five days a week, and allows participants from all over the world to buy, sell, exchange, and speculate on different currencies.

Key Features of Forex:

- Currency Pairs: In Forex trading, currencies are always traded in pairs. Each currency pair represents the value of one currency relative to another. For example, the EUR/USD pair represents the Euro against the US Dollar. The first currency in the pair is the base currency, while the second one is the quote currency.
- Over-the-Counter (OTC) Market: Forex trading is conducted over the counter, meaning there is no centralized exchange like in the stock market. Instead, trading takes place electronically through a network of banks, brokers, and financial institutions.
- Largest Financial Market: With a daily trading volume exceeding $6 trillion, the Forex market dwarfs other financial markets. Its vast size and liquidity make it highly accessible to traders of all sizes.
- High Liquidity: The Forex market's liquidity ensures that participants can buy or sell currencies quickly without significantly impacting prices. This feature allows for ease of execution and reduces the risk of market manipulation.

- Trading Hours: Forex trading is available 24 hours a day, five days a week, starting with the Asian trading session on Sunday evening and ending with the New York session on Friday evening (UTC time).
- Leverage: Forex brokers often offer leverage to traders, enabling them to control larger positions in the market with a smaller initial investment. While leverage can amplify profits, it also increases the potential for losses and requires careful risk management.

Why Trade Forex?

Forex trading attracts a diverse range of participants for various reasons:

- Speculation and Profits: Traders engage in Forex to speculate on currency price movements, aiming to profit from favorable exchange rate fluctuations.
- Hedging and Risk Management: Businesses and corporations use Forex to hedge against currency risk in their international operations, protecting themselves from adverse currency movements.
- Portfolio Diversification: Investors diversify their portfolios by including Forex investments, which can provide a hedge against fluctuations in other asset classes.
- Liquidity and Accessibility: The high liquidity and extended trading hours make Forex trading accessible to traders from different time zones and with various trading preferences.
- Low Trading Costs: The Forex market generally has low transaction costs, primarily limited to the spread (the difference between the bid and ask price) and occasional brokerage fees.

Factors Influencing Forex Prices:

The value of a currency in the Forex market is influenced by various factors, including:

- Interest Rates: Higher interest rates tend to attract foreign capital, increasing demand for the currency and potentially strengthening its value.
- Economic Indicators: Economic data, such as GDP growth, employment figures, inflation rates, and trade balances, affect a country's currency strength.
- Geopolitical Events: Political stability, geopolitical tensions, and trade relations can impact currency values.
- Central Bank Policies: Decisions made by central banks regarding monetary policies and interventions can significantly influence currency movements.
- Market Sentiment: Trader perceptions, risk appetite, and market speculation also play a role in determining Forex prices.

In conclusion, Forex is the global market where currencies are bought and sold, enabling participants to exchange one currency for another based on prevailing exchange rates. Its immense size, high liquidity, and 24-hour accessibility make it a dynamic and attractive market for traders, investors, businesses, and financial institutions seeking profit opportunities, risk management, and portfolio diversification. Understanding the factors that influence Forex prices is essential for successful trading in this fascinating and ever-evolving financial landscape.

1.2 History and Evolution of the Forex Market

The history and evolution of the Forex market can be traced back to ancient times when people engaged in currency exchange to facilitate trade between different regions. However, modern Forex trading, as we know it today, has undergone significant changes and developments over the years. Let's explore the key milestones in the history and evolution of the Forex market:

1. Ancient Times:

Currency exchange has existed for centuries, with traders and merchants exchanging different currencies to facilitate international trade. Merchants in ancient civilizations, such as the Phoenicians, Egyptians, and Greeks, engaged in early forms of Forex trading to conduct cross-border transactions.

2. The Gold Standard (19th Century):

During the 19th century, the Gold Standard was established in many countries. Under the Gold Standard, currencies were pegged to a specific amount of gold, creating a fixed exchange rate system. The value of a currency was directly linked to a specific amount of gold held by the issuing country's central bank.

3. The Bretton Woods Agreement (1944):

After World War II, the Bretton Woods Agreement was established in 1944 at a conference in Bretton Woods, New Hampshire, USA. The agreement aimed to stabilize the global financial system by pegging major currencies to the US Dollar, which was convertible to gold at a fixed rate. This fixed exchange rate system led to the creation of the International Monetary Fund (IMF) and the World Bank.

4. The Collapse of the Bretton Woods System (1971):

As global economic conditions changed, the Bretton Woods system faced challenges. The US faced economic difficulties, and other countries started to demand gold for their US Dollar reserves. In response, President Richard Nixon announced the suspension of the US Dollar's convertibility to gold in 1971, effectively ending the Bretton Woods system and ushering in a new era of floating exchange rates.

5. The Birth of Modern Forex Trading (1970s):

With the collapse of the Bretton Woods system, major currencies started to float freely against each other. This marked the beginning of modern Forex trading as we know it today. During the 1970s, technological advancements, such as computer networks and telecommunication systems, made it possible for financial institutions to exchange currencies electronically, facilitating international currency trading.

6. Introduction of Electronic Trading Platforms (1990s):

The 1990s saw significant advancements in electronic trading technology, leading to the creation of online trading platforms. These platforms allowed individual retail traders to access the Forex market and trade currencies from the comfort of their homes.

7. Globalization and Increased Participation (2000s):

With the rise of globalization, cross-border trade, and investment increased significantly, leading to a surge in Forex trading activities. The Forex market became even more accessible to retail traders, as online brokers offered competitive trading conditions and leveraged accounts.

8. High-Frequency Trading and Algorithmic Trading (2010s):

In the 2010s, high-frequency trading (HFT) and algorithmic trading became prevalent in the Forex market. HFT involves the use of sophisticated computer algorithms to execute a large number of trades in fractions of a second, taking advantage of small price discrepancies. Algorithmic trading uses pre-programmed instructions to execute trades based on predefined criteria, further increasing market efficiency.

9. Regulatory Changes and Market Oversight:

In response to the growing popularity of Forex trading and to protect investors, regulatory authorities in different countries introduced measures to ensure fair and transparent trading practices. Regulatory oversight became more comprehensive, and reputable Forex brokers obtained licenses from regulatory bodies.

10. Technological Advancements and Mobile Trading:

Recent years have seen continuous advancements in trading technology, making Forex trading more accessible than ever. Mobile trading apps and platforms have gained popularity, allowing traders to monitor and execute trades on smartphones and tablets.

The history and evolution of the Forex market demonstrate its transformation from a rudimentary currency exchange system to a vast and dynamic global financial market. Advancements in technology, changes in economic systems, and increasing global trade have shaped the Forex market into the largest and most liquid market in the world today. As the market continues to evolve, it remains an integral part of the global financial landscape, providing opportunities for individuals, institutions, and businesses to participate in international currency trading and capitalize on exchange rate fluctuations.

1.3 Major Participants in Forex Trading

The Forex market is a decentralized over-the-counter (OTC) market where currencies are bought and sold. It involves a diverse range of participants from various sectors, each with different objectives and roles. The major participants in Forex trading include:

- Banks and Financial Institutions: Banks are the primary players in the Forex market. Large international banks engage in Forex trading to facilitate foreign exchange transactions for their clients, including corporations, institutions, and governments. They also trade on their own behalf to profit from currency price movements and manage their foreign exchange reserves.

- Central Banks: Central banks play a significant role in the Forex market. They are responsible for formulating and implementing monetary policies to stabilize their country's currency and ensure economic stability. Central banks use Forex reserves to intervene in the market, influencing exchange rates and maintaining currency value.

- Corporations: Multinational corporations participate in Forex trading to hedge against currency risks resulting from their international business operations. They use Forex markets to convert profits and payments in different currencies, reducing the impact of exchange rate fluctuations on their bottom line.

- Investment Funds and Hedge Funds: Investment funds, including mutual funds and hedge funds, often engage in Forex trading as part of their overall investment strategies. These funds may trade currencies directly or use currency derivatives to speculate on currency movements or hedge their positions.

- Retail Traders: Individual retail traders are an increasingly significant segment of the Forex market. Thanks to technological advancements and online trading platforms provided by brokers, retail traders now have access to the Forex market from anywhere in the world. Retail traders aim to profit from short-term price movements or implement longer-term trading strategies.

- Brokers: Forex brokers act as intermediaries between traders and the Forex market. They provide trading platforms that allow traders to access the market, execute trades, and manage their accounts. Brokers earn revenue through spreads and commissions charged on each trade.

- Market Makers: Some large financial institutions act as market makers in the Forex market. Market makers provide liquidity by offering buy and sell quotes for currency pairs, ensuring that there is always a market available for traders to execute their trades.
- Speculators: Speculators are individuals or entities that participate in Forex trading purely to profit from price fluctuations. They may hold positions for short periods or engage in day trading to take advantage of intraday price movements.
- Governments and Sovereign Wealth Funds: Besides central banks, governments, and sovereign wealth funds may also participate in Forex trading. Governments may engage in currency intervention to stabilize their currency's value, while sovereign wealth funds may use Forex trading as part of their investment strategies.
- Commercial and Investment Banks: Apart from major international banks, commercial and investment banks engage in Forex trading to serve their corporate clients and institutional investors' foreign exchange needs.

The diversity of participants in the Forex market contributes to its high liquidity, continuous trading hours, and the availability of trading opportunities. Each participant brings a unique perspective and motive to the market, creating a dynamic and ever-changing financial landscape that offers ample possibilities for profit and risk management.

1.4 Key Currency Pairs

Key currency pairs, also known as major currency pairs, are the most traded and widely recognized currency pairs in the Forex market. These pairs involve the currencies of the world's largest and most influential economies. Key currency pairs account for the majority of trading volume and are considered the most liquid and stable pairs, making them popular among traders and investors. The main key currency pairs include:

- EUR/USD (Euro/US Dollar): The EUR/USD is the most traded and liquid currency pair in the Forex market. It represents the Euro, the currency of the European Union, against the US Dollar, the world's primary reserve currency. This pair is often influenced by economic data, interest rate decisions, and political developments in both the Eurozone and the United States.
- USD/JPY (US Dollar/Japanese Yen): The USD/JPY is the second most traded currency pair and represents the US Dollar against the Japanese Yen. Japan is a major global economy, and the Japanese Yen is considered a safe-haven currency. Factors affecting this pair include economic indicators, interest rate differentials, and market sentiment.
- GBP/USD (British Pound/US Dollar): The GBP/USD pair represents the British Pound Sterling against the US Dollar. It is commonly known as the "Cable," a nickname derived from the transatlantic communication cable that was used to transmit exchange rates between London and New York. This pair is influenced by UK economic data, Brexit developments, and US economic indicators.
- USD/CHF (US Dollar/Swiss Franc): The USD/CHF pair represents the US Dollar against the Swiss Franc, the currency of Switzerland. Switzerland's reputation as a stable and safe-haven economy influences this pair. Additionally, the Swiss National Bank's monetary policies and interventions may impact the exchange rate.
- USD/CAD (US Dollar/Canadian Dollar): The USD/CAD pair represents the US Dollar against the Canadian Dollar, also known

as the "Loonie." Canada is a major oil exporter, and the pair is influenced by crude oil prices, economic data from both countries and changes in interest rates.

- AUD/USD (Australian Dollar/US Dollar): The AUD/USD pair represents the Australian Dollar against the US Dollar. Australia's economy is closely tied to commodity prices, particularly metals, and minerals, making this pair sensitive to global commodity trends and economic developments in China, Australia's major trading partner.

- NZD/USD (New Zealand Dollar/US Dollar): The NZD/USD pair represents the New Zealand Dollar against the US Dollar. Similar to the AUD/USD pair, this currency pair is influenced by commodity prices and economic data from both countries.

These seven currency pairs are considered the key currency pairs due to their high liquidity, consistent trading volumes, and significant impact on the global financial markets. Traders and investors closely monitor these pairs to gain insights into the health and direction of the world's major economies and to identify potential trading opportunities. As a result, they are frequently used in various trading strategies and analytical studies within the Forex market.

Chapter 2: Decoding the Forex Market

In this chapter, we will delve deeper into understanding the Forex market and its intricate workings. Decoding the Forex market involves grasping the essential concepts, tools, and analysis methods that enable traders to make informed decisions and navigate the complexities of currency trading successfully. We will explore the following key aspects:

1. Fundamental Analysis:

Fundamental analysis is a crucial tool in decoding the Forex market. We will explore how economic indicators, such as GDP, inflation rates, employment data, and central bank policies, influence currency values. Understanding the impact of geopolitical events, trade relations, and global economic trends will be essential in making well-informed trading decisions based on fundamental analysis.

2. Technical Analysis:

Technical analysis involves studying historical price charts, patterns, and indicators to forecast future price movements. We will dive into various technical analysis tools, such as moving averages, support and resistance levels, Fibonacci retracements, and oscillators. Decoding technical analysis will enable traders to identify trends, reversals, and potential entry and exit points in the Forex market.

3. Candlestick Charting:

Candlestick charting is a widely used method in technical analysis. We will explore the anatomy of candlestick patterns, including doji, engulfing patterns, hammers, and shooting stars. Decoding candlestick charting will equip traders with the ability to interpret price action and make informed decisions based on candlestick patterns.

4. Risk Management Strategies:

Decoding the Forex market involves understanding the importance of risk management. We will explore various risk management strategies, including position sizing, setting stop-loss and take-profit levels, and diversification. Implementing effective risk management techniques will help traders preserve their capital and protect their profits.

5. Trading Psychology:

Emotions play a significant role in Forex trading. Decoding trading psychology will involve understanding the impact of fear, greed, and overconfidence on trading decisions. We will explore techniques to maintain emotional discipline, build resilience, and cultivate a rational mindset for successful trading.

6. Currency Correlations:

Currency pairs are not isolated entities in the Forex market. Understanding currency correlations will be crucial in deciding how certain currency pairs interact with others and how external factors can affect multiple currency pairs simultaneously. We will explore positive and negative correlations and how they can influence trading strategies.

7. Trading Strategies and Styles:

Decoding the Forex market will involve exploring different trading strategies and styles. From day trading to swing trading and long-term investing, understanding various approaches will help traders identify the best-fit strategy based on their risk tolerance and trading goals.

8. News Trading and Economic Calendar:

News and economic events can cause significant market volatility. We will explore the art of news trading and how traders can use economic calendars to stay informed about upcoming events that may impact currency markets. Decoding news trading will enable traders to react effectively to market-moving events.

9. Backtesting and Trading Plans:

Decoding the Forex market also involves thorough preparation. We will explore the importance of backtesting trading strategies and developing well-structured trading plans. Backtesting historical data will help validate strategies before implementing them in live markets, while trading plans will provide a clear roadmap for consistent and disciplined trading.

10. Advanced Trading Tools and Indicators:

Decoding the Forex market will introduce traders to advanced trading tools and indicators that can enhance their analysis. We will explore tools such as automated trading systems (Expert Advisors), sentiment analysis, and pattern recognition software.

Decoding the Forex market is a multifaceted process that requires a comprehensive understanding of fundamental and technical analysis, risk management, trading psychology, and various trading strategies. Armed with this knowledge, traders can approach the Forex market with confidence, make informed decisions, and adapt to the dynamic and ever-changing nature of currency trading. In the subsequent chapters of this book, we will explore each aspect in detail, providing practical insights and real-life examples to empower traders with the skills and expertise needed for success in the Forex market.

2.1 Fundamental Analysis

Fundamental analysis is a method used to evaluate the intrinsic value of an asset, such as a currency in the case of the Forex market, by analyzing relevant economic, financial, and geopolitical factors. This analysis aims to understand the underlying forces that influence supply and demand and ultimately determine the asset's true value. In the context of the Forex market, fundamental analysis involves studying various economic indicators, central bank policies, geopolitical events, and other fundamental factors that impact the strength and stability of a country's currency.

Key Components of Fundamental Analysis in Forex:

- Economic Indicators: Economic indicators are essential data points that provide insights into a country's economic health. These indicators include Gross Domestic Product (GDP), inflation rates (Consumer Price Index - CPI), employment data (unemployment rate, non-farm payrolls), industrial production, retail sales, and trade balances (imports and exports). Traders monitor these indicators to assess the economic performance of a country and its potential impact on the currency's value.
- Interest Rates and Monetary Policy: Central banks play a vital role in setting interest rates and implementing monetary policies. Changes in interest rates can significantly influence a currency's value. Higher interest rates tend to attract foreign investment, strengthening the currency, while lower interest rates may lead to capital outflows, weakening the currency. Traders closely follow central bank meetings and policy statements to gauge potential interest rate changes and future policy direction.
- Geopolitical Events and News: Geopolitical events, such as elections, political instability, trade disputes, and international conflicts, can have a substantial impact on currency markets. Unforeseen events and news announcements can cause sharp movements in currency pairs, making it essential for traders to stay updated on global political developments.
- Market Sentiment and Risk Appetite: Market sentiment and risk appetite refer to the overall perception and confidence of market participants. Positive sentiment and risk appetite often lead to

increased demand for higher-yielding currencies, while risk aversion tends to favor safe-haven currencies.

Tools and Methods in Fundamental Analysis:

- Economic Calendars: Traders use economic calendars to track the release schedule of key economic indicators and other significant events. Economic calendars help traders plan their trades and anticipate potential market-moving events.
- Central Bank Statements: Statements and press conferences from central banks, especially from major economies like the US Federal Reserve, European Central Bank (ECB), and Bank of Japan (BOJ), can provide valuable insights into future monetary policy decisions.
- Country-Specific News Sources: Traders monitor news sources specific to the countries whose currencies they are trading. Local news can provide insights into economic, political, and social factors that may impact currency values.
- Correlation Analysis: Fundamental analysis includes understanding how economic factors influence currency pairs. Traders often use correlation analysis to determine how closely two currency pairs move in relation to each other, allowing them to spot potential trading opportunities or risks.

Strengths and Limitations of Fundamental Analysis:

1. **Strengths:**

- Provides a comprehensive understanding of the underlying factors impacting currency values.
- Can identify long-term trends and fundamental shifts in the Forex market.
- Useful for long-term investors and traders who consider macroeconomic factors.

2. Limitations:

- Requires extensive research and analysis, which can be time-consuming.
- Short-term price movements may not always align with fundamental factors.
- Market sentiment and speculative activities can temporarily override fundamental analysis.

Fundamental analysis is a valuable tool for Forex traders seeking to understand the fundamental drivers of currency prices. By analyzing economic indicators, central bank policies, geopolitical events, and market sentiment, traders can make informed decisions and develop a comprehensive outlook on currency pairs. Combining fundamental analysis with technical analysis and risk management strategies empowers traders to navigate the Forex market with a holistic approach, aiming for profitable and well-informed trading decisions.

1.2 Technical Analysis

Technical analysis is a method used to evaluate and predict future price movements in financial markets, including the Forex market, by analyzing historical price data and market statistics. Traders who use technical analysis, often referred to as "chartists," study price charts and apply various tools and indicators to identify patterns, trends, support and resistance levels, and other key factors that can help them make trading decisions.

Key Components of Technical Analysis in Forex:

- Price Charts: Price charts are the foundation of technical analysis. Traders use different types of charts, such as line charts, bar charts, and candlestick charts, to visualize historical price movements and identify patterns and trends.
- Trends: Technical analysis focuses on identifying trends in price movements. Trends can be upward (bullish), downward (bearish), or sideways (consolidation). Traders use trendlines and moving averages to determine the direction and strength of a trend.
- Support and Resistance Levels: Support levels are price levels where the currency pair tends to find buying interest and reverse its downward movement. Resistance levels are price levels where selling interest tends to emerge, causing the pair to reverse its upward movement. Identifying support and resistance levels is crucial for determining potential entry and exit points.
- Technical Indicators: Technical indicators are mathematical calculations based on historical price and volume data. They provide additional insights into market trends, momentum, and potential reversal points. Common technical indicators in Forex

include Moving Averages (MA), Relative Strength Index (RSI), Moving Average Convergence Divergence (MACD), and Bollinger Bands.

- Chart Patterns: Chart patterns are distinctive formations that appear on price charts and indicate potential future price movements. Common chart patterns in technical analysis include head and shoulders, double tops and bottoms, triangles, and flags.
- Fibonacci Retracements: Fibonacci retracements are based on the Fibonacci sequence and are used to identify potential support and resistance levels based on specific price ratios. Traders often use Fibonacci retracements to assess the strength of a trend and find potential reversal points.

Tools and Methods in Technical Analysis:

- Trendlines: Trendlines are drawn on price charts to connect higher lows in an uptrend or lower highs in a downtrend. They help traders identify the direction and strength of a trend.
- Moving Averages: Moving averages smooth out price data over a specific period and help identify the overall trend direction. Traders use simple moving averages (SMA) and exponential moving averages (EMA) to identify trend changes.
- Candlestick Patterns: Candlestick patterns provide valuable insights into price action and market sentiment. Patterns such as doji, engulfing, and hammer can indicate potential reversals or continuations in price movements.
- Support and Resistance Analysis: Traders use horizontal lines on price charts to identify support and resistance levels, helping them make decisions about entry and exit points.

Strengths and Limitations of Technical Analysis:

1. Strengths:

- Provides clear and visual insights into historical price movements and patterns.
- Helps traders identify trends, potential entry and exit points, and stop-loss levels.
- Can be applied to various timeframes, making it suitable for both short-term and long-term traders.

2. Limitations:

- Technical analysis does not consider fundamental factors that may impact currency values.
- Over-reliance on technical indicators can lead to false signals and misinterpretations.
- Market sentiment and unforeseen events can override technical analysis predictions.

Technical analysis is a valuable tool for Forex traders seeking to understand and predict price movements based on historical data and market patterns. By analyzing price charts, trends, technical indicators, and chart patterns, traders can make informed decisions and develop trading strategies. Integrating technical analysis with other analysis methods, such as fundamental analysis and risk management, allows traders to approach the Forex market with a comprehensive and well-rounded approach, aiming for profitable and successful trading outcomes.

2.3 Sentiment Analysis

Sentiment analysis, also known as market sentiment analysis or trader sentiment analysis, is a method used in Forex trading to gauge the overall sentiment or mood of market participants towards a particular currency or the entire Forex market. It involves assessing the collective emotions and beliefs of traders and investors to understand how they perceive the market's future direction. Sentiment analysis is an essential tool for traders seeking to complement fundamental and technical analysis with insights into the psychological aspects of trading.

Key Components of Sentiment Analysis in Forex:

- Bullish Sentiment: Bullish sentiment refers to a positive outlook on the market or a specific currency. Traders and investors feel optimistic, expecting prices to rise or an uptrend to continue. Bullish sentiment can lead to increased buying activity and demand for a currency.
- Bearish Sentiment: Bearish sentiment indicates a negative outlook on the market or a particular currency. Traders and investors feel pessimistic, anticipating price declines or a continuation of a downtrend. Bearish sentiment can lead to increased selling activity and a higher supply of a currency.
- Market Sentiment Indicators: Sentiment analysis often employs market sentiment indicators that measure the ratio of bullish to bearish traders or the overall sentiment among market participants. These indicators can be proprietary sentiment indicators provided by brokers or sentiment gauges based on traders' positioning in the market.

- Contrarian Approach: Contrarian traders use sentiment analysis to take positions opposite to the prevailing sentiment. For example, if the majority of traders are bullish on a currency, a contrarian trader might consider taking a bearish position, expecting a potential reversal in price.

Tools and Methods in Sentiment Analysis:

- Commitments of Traders (COT) Report: The COT report, published by regulatory authorities, provides insights into the positioning of large traders, such as commercial traders, speculators, and hedgers. Analyzing the COT report can offer valuable information about the sentiment of major market players.
- Trader Surveys: Some financial institutions and research firms conduct trader sentiment surveys to gauge the opinions and outlook of individual traders and investors. These surveys provide sentiment data that can be analyzed by Forex traders.
- Social Media and News Monitoring: Sentiment analysis can involve monitoring social media platforms and financial news sources to gauge the general sentiment among traders and investors. Social media discussions and news sentiment can influence market behavior.

Strengths and Limitations of Sentiment Analysis:

Strengths:

- Provides insights into traders' collective emotions and beliefs, which can influence market movements.
- Can help identify potential market reversals and turning points based on extreme sentiment conditions.
- Complements other forms of analysis, such as fundamental and technical analysis, for a more comprehensive trading strategy.

Limitations:

- Sentiment analysis is subjective and can be influenced by individual biases and opinions.
- Sentiment indicators can sometimes provide conflicting signals, making interpretation challenging.
- Traders should be cautious of excessive reliance on sentiment analysis alone, as market sentiment can change quickly and unpredictably.

Sentiment analysis is a valuable tool for Forex traders seeking to gain insights into the psychology of the market and potential shifts in market sentiment. By assessing the collective feelings and beliefs of market participants, traders can better understand market dynamics and potential price movements. Combining sentiment analysis with fundamental and technical analysis can provide a more comprehensive approach to Forex trading, helping traders make informed decisions and manage risks effectively in the dynamic and ever-changing Forex market.

2.4 Intermarket Analysis

Intermarket analysis is a method used in financial markets, including the Forex market, to study the relationships and interactions between different asset classes. It involves analyzing the interdependencies and correlations among various markets, such as stocks, bonds, commodities, and currencies, to gain insights into potential price movements and trends. The goal of Intermarket analysis is to identify connections between different markets that can help traders make more informed decisions and develop a broader understanding of the overall market environment.

Key Concepts of Intermarket Analysis in Forex:

- Intermarket Relationships: Intermarket analysis explores how different asset classes influence and impact each other. For example, changes in interest rates (bond market) can affect the value of a country's currency (Forex market), and fluctuations in commodity prices can influence the economies of commodity-exporting countries and their respective currencies.
- Risk-On and Risk-Off Sentiment: Intermarket analysis often involves examining the risk-on and risk-off sentiment in financial markets. During risk-on sentiment, investors are more willing to take on risk, leading to higher demand for riskier assets like stocks and high-yielding currencies. Conversely, during risk-off sentiment, investors seek safer assets, such as bonds and safe-haven currencies like the US Dollar and Japanese Yen.
- Commodity Prices and Currency Relationships: Certain currencies, especially those of commodity-exporting countries, have close correlations with commodity prices. For example, the Canadian

Dollar (CAD) tends to move in tandem with oil prices due to Canada's significant oil exports. Similarly, the Australian Dollar (AUD) and New Zealand Dollar (NZD) are often influenced by commodity prices like gold and agricultural products.

Tools and Methods in Intermarket Analysis:

- Correlation Analysis: Intermarket analysis often involves assessing correlations between different asset classes and currency pairs. Positive correlations mean that two assets tend to move in the same direction, while negative correlations mean they move in opposite directions.
- Commodity Prices: Traders monitor commodity prices, such as oil, gold, and copper, to understand their potential impact on currencies. Commodity prices can influence inflation, trade balances, and economic growth, affecting currency values.
- Interest Rates and Bonds: Interest rates and bond yields are critical components of Intermarket analysis. Changes in interest rates can affect capital flows, leading to currency appreciation or depreciation.

Strengths and Limitations of Intermarket Analysis:

Strengths:

- Provides a broader understanding of the financial markets and potential interrelationships between different asset classes.

- Helps traders anticipate potential shifts in market sentiment and identify possible trading opportunities.
- Complements other forms of analysis, such as fundamental and technical analysis, for a more comprehensive trading approach.

Limitations:

- Intermarket relationships can be complex and may change over time.
- Correlations between asset classes may not always be stable or reliable.
- The Intermarket analysis does not replace other types of analysis but should be used as part of a broader trading strategy.

Intermarket analysis is a valuable tool for Forex traders seeking to understand the interconnectedness of different financial markets and their potential impact on currency movements. By studying the relationships between stocks, bonds, commodities, and currencies, traders can gain valuable insights into market sentiment and potential trading opportunities. Integrating intermarket analysis with other analysis methods, such as fundamental analysis, technical analysis, and sentiment analysis, allows traders to develop a comprehensive and well-informed approach to Forex trading, increasing the likelihood of successful trading outcomes.

Chapter 3: Building a Strong Foundation

In this chapter, we will focus on building a solid foundation for successful Forex trading. A strong foundation is essential for navigating the complexities of the Forex market with confidence and achieving consistent profits. We will cover the following key elements to establish a robust trading groundwork:

1. Setting Clear Goals:

Before diving into Forex trading, it's crucial to set clear and realistic goals. Define your financial objectives, risk tolerance, and preferred trading style (e.g., day trading, swing trading, or long-term investing). Having well-defined goals will help you stay focused and make informed decisions aligned with your trading objectives.

2. Understanding Risk Management:

Risk management is a fundamental pillar of successful trading. Learn how to manage your capital effectively and determine position sizes that align with your risk tolerance. Implementing stop-loss and take-profit orders will safeguard your trades and help you maintain discipline during market fluctuations.

3. Selecting the Right Broker:

Choosing the right Forex broker is critical for a positive trading experience. Research different brokers, considering factors such as regulation, trading platforms, fees, spreads, leverage, and customer support. A reputable and reliable broker is essential for executing trades efficiently and securely.

4. Learning Trading Psychology:

Trading psychology plays a significant role in your success as a trader. Develop emotional discipline and control fear, greed, and impulsiveness. Understand the psychological aspects of trading and learn techniques to maintain a positive and rational mindset during both winning and losing trades.

5. Mastering Technical Analysis:

Technical analysis is a powerful tool for understanding price movements and identifying trading opportunities. Learn how to read price charts, recognize patterns, use technical indicators effectively, and draw support and resistance levels. Technical analysis will help you make informed entry and exit decisions.

6. Embracing Fundamental Analysis:

Fundamental analysis is essential for understanding the underlying drivers of currency movements. Familiarize yourself with economic indicators, central bank policies, geopolitical events, and how they influence currency values. Combining fundamental analysis with technical analysis will provide a comprehensive perspective on the market.

7. Practicing with Demo Accounts:

Before risking real money, practice trading strategies and techniques with demo accounts. Demo accounts offer a risk-free environment to gain experience, test different approaches, and refine your trading skills.

8. Developing a Trading Plan:

Create a well-structured trading plan that outlines your trading goals, strategies, risk management rules, and trading routine. Your trading plan will serve as a roadmap and keep you focused on your trading objectives.

9. Staying Informed and Adapting:

Stay updated on financial news, economic events, and market developments that may impact currency movements. Remain adaptable to changing market conditions and be willing to adjust your strategies when necessary.

10. Keeping Records and Analyzing Performance:

Maintain a trading journal to record all your trades and analyze your performance regularly. Assess your strengths and weaknesses, learn from past trades, and make improvements to enhance your trading skills.

Building a strong foundation is crucial for achieving long-term success in Forex trading. By setting clear goals, managing risk, mastering technical and fundamental analysis, and developing a disciplined trading psychology, you will be better equipped to navigate the challenges of the Forex market. Continuously learning, practicing, and staying informed will help you adapt to market dynamics and refine your trading strategies. In the next chapters of this book, we will delve deeper into various trading techniques and advanced strategies to further enhance your Forex trading expertise.

3.1 Setting Up a Forex Trading Account

Setting up a Forex trading account is a straightforward process, and it involves several steps to ensure you have a platform to participate in the Forex market. Follow these steps to set up your Forex trading account:

1. **Research and Choose a Reputable Broker:**

Start by researching different Forex brokers to find a reputable and regulated one. Look for brokers with a good track record, competitive spreads, reliable trading platforms, and excellent customer support. Ensure that the broker is regulated by a recognized financial authority for added security.

2. Register with the Chosen Broker:

Once you've selected a broker, visit their website and click on the "Open Account" or "Register" button. You'll be directed to an online application form.

3. Complete the Account Application Form:

Fill out the required information on the account application form. This typically includes personal details such as your name, address, date of birth, email address, and phone number. You may also need to provide identification documents to verify your identity, such as a passport or driver's license, and proof of address, such as a utility bill or bank statement.

4. Choose the Account Type:

Select the type of Forex trading account that suits your trading preferences and needs. Brokers often offer various account types, such as standard accounts, mini accounts, or Islamic accounts (swap-free accounts for those adhering to Islamic principles). Consider factors like minimum deposit requirements, leverage, and spreads when choosing an account type.

5. Fund Your Account:

After completing the account application and verification process, fund your trading account with the minimum required deposit. Brokers offer various deposit methods, such as credit/debit cards, bank transfers, e-wallets, or other online payment options. Choose the method that is most convenient and secure for you.

6. Download and Set Up Trading Platform:

Once your account is funded, download and install the trading platform provided by your broker. Most brokers offer popular platforms like MetaTrader 4 (MT4) or MetaTrader 5 (MT5). These platforms offer comprehensive charting tools, technical indicators, and a user-friendly interface for executing trades.

7. Log In and Start Trading:

Once your trading platform is set up, log in with your account credentials and start trading. Familiarize yourself with the platform's features, tools, and order execution process. You can start by using a demo account to practice trading strategies without risking real money.

8. Implement Risk Management:

Before placing trades, establish risk management rules to protect your capital. Set stop-loss and take-profit levels for each trade and determine the appropriate position size based on your risk tolerance. Implementing risk management is essential to safeguard your trading account from excessive losses.

9. Stay Informed and Continuously Learn:

Stay updated on financial news, economic events, and market developments that may impact currency prices. Continuously learn and improve your trading skills through books, courses, webinars, and other educational resources.

10. Keep Trading Journal:

Maintain a trading journal to record your trades, including entry and exit points, the reasoning behind each trade, and the outcome. Regularly analyze your trading journal to identify patterns, strengths, and areas for improvement.

Setting up a Forex trading account involves choosing a reputable broker, completing an account application, funding your account, and setting up the trading platform. It's crucial to practice risk management, continuously learn, and stay informed to make informed trading decisions. By following these steps and adopting a disciplined approach to trading, you can begin your Forex trading journey with confidence and increase your chances of success in the dynamic and exciting world of Forex trading.

3.2 Risk Management Strategies

Risk management strategies are essential tools for protecting your trading capital and minimizing potential losses in Forex trading. By implementing effective risk management techniques, you can enhance the longevity of your trading account and increase the likelihood of achieving consistent profits. Here are some key risk management strategies to consider:

1. **Position Sizing:**

Position sizing refers to determining the appropriate amount of capital to risk on each trade. It is crucial to avoid overexposure to any single trade, as this could lead to significant losses if the trade goes against you. A common rule of thumb is to risk only a small percentage (e.g., 1% to 2%) of your total trading capital on any given trade.

2. **Stop-Loss Orders:**

A stop-loss order is an essential risk management tool that allows you to preset the maximum amount you are willing to lose on a trade. Placing a stop-loss order ensures that your position is automatically closed if the market moves against you, helping to limit potential losses.

3. **Take-Profit Orders:**

Take-profit orders allow you to lock in profits by setting a predetermined target level for exiting a profitable trade. By setting a take-profit order, you can avoid the temptation to hold onto winning trades for too long, potentially giving back gains if the market reverses.

4. Risk-Reward Ratio:

The risk-reward ratio compares the potential profit of a trade to the potential loss. A favorable risk-reward ratio ensures that the potential reward is higher than the potential risk. For example, aiming for a risk-reward ratio of 1:2 means you are willing to risk $1 to potentially make $2.

5. Diversification:

Diversifying your trading portfolio involves spreading your capital across multiple trades and different currency pairs. Diversification can help reduce the impact of losses on any single trade and improve the overall risk-adjusted returns.

6. Avoiding Overtrading:

Overtrading, or taking too many trades in a short period, can increase transaction costs and lead to impulsive and emotional decision-making. Stick to your trading plan and only execute trades that meet your predefined criteria.

7. Using Leverage Wisely:

Leverage can amplify both profits and losses. While it can enhance potential gains, it also increases the risk of significant losses. Use leverage cautiously and be aware of the potential impact on your trading account.

8. Risk Tolerance and Psychology:

Understanding your risk tolerance is vital in managing emotions and making rational trading decisions. Avoid trading with money you cannot afford to lose, and do not let fear or greed drive your trading choices.

9. Reviewing and Adjusting:

Regularly review your trading performance and risk management strategies. Identify areas of improvement and adjust your risk management approach as needed. Be flexible and adapt to changing market conditions.

10. Keep Emotions in Check:

Emotional discipline is crucial in risk management. Stick to your trading plan, even if you experience consecutive losses. Avoid revenge trading after a loss, as this can lead to impulsive decisions and further losses.

Risk management strategies are fundamental to successful Forex trading. By implementing position sizing, stop-loss, and take-profit orders, risk-reward ratios, diversification, and wise leverage usage, you can protect your trading capital and improve your chances of achieving consistent profits. Additionally, maintaining emotional discipline and regularly reviewing your trading performance will help you stay on track and navigate the Forex market with confidence and resilience. Remember that managing risk is an ongoing process, and continuously refining your risk management techniques is an essential aspect of becoming a skilled and profitable Forex trader.

3.3 Developing a Trading Plan

Developing a comprehensive trading plan is a critical step in becoming a successful Forex trader. A well-structured trading plan outlines your trading goals, strategies, risk management rules, and guidelines for decision-making. It serves as a roadmap that keeps you focused, disciplined, and consistent in your trading approach. Here are the key components to consider when developing your trading plan:

1. **Trading Goals:**

Start by defining your trading goals. Determine your financial objectives, such as the amount of profit you aim to achieve and the time frame for reaching your goals. Your trading goals should be specific, measurable, achievable, relevant, and time-bound (SMART).

2. **Trading Style and Strategies:**

Choose a trading style that aligns with your personality, schedule, and risk tolerance. Decide whether you will be a day trader, swing trader, or position trader. Identify the Forex trading strategies you will use, such as trend following, breakout trading, or range trading. Describe how you will implement these strategies in your plan.

3. Risk Management Rules:

Establish clear risk management rules to protect your trading capital. Define the maximum percentage of your capital you are willing to risk on each trade (e.g., 1% to 2%). Set stop-loss levels for each trade to limit potential losses and determine take-profit levels to lock in profits.

4. Money Management:

Outline your money management principles in the trading plan. Describe how you will allocate your capital among different trades and currency pairs. Consider diversification to spread risk and avoid overexposure to any single trade.

5. Trading Instruments:

Specify the currency pairs or instruments you will trade. Consider factors such as liquidity, volatility, and spreads when selecting the currency pairs to trade.

6. Entry and Exit Criteria:

Define the criteria for entering and exiting trades. Describe the technical or fundamental factors that will trigger your entry into a trade. Determine the conditions under which you will exit a trade, either by reaching a predetermined take-profit level or if the trade hits the stop-loss.

7. Trading Hours and Frequency:

Decide on your trading hours and the frequency of your trades. Consider whether you will be an active trader, monitoring the market throughout the day, or a more passive trader, entering trades based on longer-term trends.

8. Trading Platform and Tools:

Specify the trading platform and technical analysis tools you will use for executing trades and conducting market analysis. Familiarize yourself with the platform and tools to maximize their effectiveness.

9. Trading Journal:

Include a trading journal in your plan. Use it to record all your trades, including entry and exit points, the rationale behind each trade, and the outcome. Regularly review your trading journal to analyze your performance and identify areas for improvement.

10. Review and Adjustments:

A trading plan is not set in stone. Regularly review your plan and make adjustments as needed based on changing market conditions or your trading performance. Continuous improvement and adaptation are essential for long-term success.

Developing a trading plan is crucial for becoming a disciplined and successful Forex trader. By outlining your trading goals, strategies, risk management rules, and decision-making criteria, you create a structured approach to your trading activities. Stick to your trading plan, maintain emotional discipline, and continuously learn from your trading experiences to refine your strategies and improve your trading skills over time. Remember that a well-executed trading plan is a key factor in achieving consistent profits in the dynamic and challenging Forex market.

3.4 Maintaining Discipline in Forex Trading

Maintaining discipline is one of the most crucial aspects of successful Forex trading. Discipline is the ability to adhere to your trading plan, risk management rules, and emotional control, even in the face of market fluctuations and unexpected events. By maintaining discipline, you can make rational and informed trading decisions, minimize emotional trading mistakes, and increase the likelihood of consistent profits. Here are some key strategies to help you maintain discipline in Forex trading:

1. Stick to Your Trading Plan:

Follow your trading plan rigorously. Your trading plan outlines your trading goals, strategies, risk management rules, and entry and exit criteria. By adhering to your plan, you avoid impulsive trades based on emotions and stay focused on your long-term objectives.

2. Implement Risk Management:

Never risk more than a predetermined percentage of your trading capital on any single trade. Set stop-loss orders to limit potential losses, and use take-profit orders to secure profits. Risk management is vital for protecting your capital and preserving your trading account.

3. Avoid Overtrading:

Resist the temptation to overtrade or take excessive trades. Stick to high-quality setups that align with your trading plan and strategies. Overtrading can lead to increased transaction costs and emotional exhaustion.

4. Embrace Patience:

Be patient and wait for the right trading opportunities. Avoid chasing trades or entering the market out of boredom. Successful trading often requires waiting for favorable conditions to present themselves.

5. Manage Your Emotions:

Recognize and manage your emotions while trading. Fear and greed are common emotional drivers in Forex trading. Avoid making trading decisions based on these emotions and remain objective in your analysis.

6.   Control Loss Aversion:

Loss aversion is the tendency to hold onto losing positions in the hope that they will reverse. Accept that losses are a natural part of trading and be willing to cut losing trades based on your predetermined stop-loss levels.

7.   Learn from Mistakes:

Acknowledge and learn from your trading mistakes. Keeping a trading journal can help you analyze past trades and identify patterns of success and failure. Use this information to improve your trading strategies and decision-making.

8.   Set Realistic Expectations:

Set realistic expectations about the potential profits and risks of Forex trading. Avoid unrealistic promises or chasing "get-rich-quick" schemes. Understand that trading requires time, effort, and continuous learning.

9.   Take Breaks and Rest:

Trading can be mentally and emotionally taxing. Take breaks, get adequate rest, and avoid trading when you are fatigued or under stress. A clear and focused mind is essential for making sound trading decisions.

10. Continuous Learning:

Stay informed and continuously learn about Forex trading and the financial markets. Education and knowledge are empowering and can improve your confidence in your trading decisions.

Maintaining discipline in Forex trading is essential for long-term success. By sticking to your trading plan, implementing risk management, avoiding emotional trading, and continuously learning from your experiences, you can develop the emotional discipline needed to navigate the ups and downs of the Forex market. Remember that discipline is a skill that can be cultivated with practice and self-awareness. With a disciplined approach, you can become a more confident and successful Forex trader over time.

Chapter 4: Forex Trading Strategies

In this chapter, we will explore various Forex trading strategies that traders use to analyze the market and make informed trading decisions. Each strategy has its unique approach and methodology, catering to different trading styles and objectives. Understanding these strategies will help you develop a well-rounded trading toolkit. Here are some popular Forex trading strategies:

1. Trend Following Strategy:

The trend-following strategy aims to identify and ride existing market trends. Traders using this approach look for currency pairs that are trending strongly in one direction and enter trades in the direction of the trend. Technical indicators like moving averages, trendlines, and the Average Directional Index (ADX) are often used to confirm and follow trends.

2. Breakout Strategy:

The breakout strategy involves identifying key support and resistance levels and entering trades when the price breaks out of these levels. Breakouts can indicate potential trend reversals or the continuation of existing trends. Traders use technical tools like Bollinger Bands and Donchian Channels to spot breakout opportunities.

3. Range Trading Strategy:

Range trading involves identifying currency pairs that are trading within a defined range, bounded by support and resistance levels. Traders buy at support and sell at resistance, capitalizing on price oscillations within the range. Oscillators like the Relative Strength Index (RSI) and the Stochastic Oscillator can help traders identify overbought and oversold conditions.

4. Carry Trade Strategy:

The carry trade strategy capitalizes on interest rate differentials between currency pairs. Traders buy currencies with higher interest rates and sell currencies with lower interest rates. By holding the higher-yielding currency, traders aim to earn interest rate differentials over time.

5. News Trading Strategy:

News trading involves trading around significant economic events and news releases that can cause high market volatility. Traders monitor economic calendars and enter positions before or after major news announcements, aiming to profit from rapid price movements.

6. Scalping Strategy:

Scalping is a short-term trading strategy that involves making numerous quick trades to profit from small price movements. Scalpers often hold positions for seconds to minutes, aiming to accumulate small gains over time. Tight spreads and low commissions are essential for successful scalping.

7. Carry Grid Strategy:

The carry grid strategy is a combination of the carry trade and grid trading strategies. It involves creating a grid of buy and sell orders around a central price level. Traders earn interest rate differentials while taking advantage of price fluctuations within the grid.

8. Price Action Strategy:

The price action strategy relies on reading and analyzing pure price movements without using indicators. Traders interpret candlestick patterns, chart patterns, and support and resistance levels to make trading decisions.

9. Fibonacci Strategy:

The Fibonacci strategy uses Fibonacci retracement and extension levels to identify potential support and resistance levels and predict price targets. Traders use Fibonacci tools alongside other technical indicators to spot trading opportunities.

10. Harmonic Pattern Strategy:

The harmonic pattern strategy involves identifying specific chart patterns with distinct Fibonacci ratios. These patterns, such as the Gartley, Butterfly, and Bat patterns, offer potential entry and exit points based on the completion of harmonic structures.

Forex trading strategies provide traders with a diverse range of techniques to analyze the market and execute trades. Each strategy offers its advantages and considerations, catering to different trading styles and risk appetites. It's essential to understand the strengths and limitations of each strategy and choose the one that aligns with your trading goals and preferences. Combining multiple strategies and adjusting your approach based on market conditions can help you develop a versatile and effective trading methodology in the dynamic world of Forex trading.

4.1 Day Trading Strategies

Day trading is a popular trading style that involves opening and closing positions within the same trading day. Day traders aim to profit from short-term price movements and typically do not hold positions overnight. This strategy requires quick decision-making, discipline, and the ability to manage risk effectively. Here are some common day trading strategies used by Forex traders:

1. Scalping:

Scalping is a high-frequency trading strategy where traders make numerous small trades throughout the day to capitalize on tiny price movements. Scalpers aim to make a small profit on each trade, relying on the sheer volume of trades to accumulate profits. Scalping requires quick execution, tight spreads, and low trading costs.

2. Momentum Trading:

Momentum trading involves trading in the direction of a strong price trend. Traders look for currency pairs with significant momentum and enter trades as the trend gains strength. Technical indicators like moving averages, the Relative Strength Index (RSI), and the Moving Average Convergence Divergence (MACD) are commonly used to identify momentum.

3. Range Trading:

Range trading is suitable when the market is trading within a defined range. Traders buy at support levels and sell at resistance levels, profiting from price oscillations within the range. Range trading requires patience and the ability to identify reliable support and resistance levels.

4. Breakout Trading:

Breakout traders aim to profit from price movements that occur when the price breaks above or below key support or resistance levels. They enter trades when the price breaks out of the range, expecting a continuation of the breakout trend. Traders use technical indicators to confirm breakouts and manage risk effectively.

5. News Trading:

News trading involves trading around major economic news releases and events that can cause significant market volatility. Traders analyze economic calendars and enter positions before or after news announcements to profit from rapid price movements.

6. Pivot Point Strategy:

Pivot points are key price levels based on the previous day's high, low, and closing prices. Traders use pivot points to identify potential support and resistance levels. They enter trades when the price approaches pivot points, expecting a bounce or breakout.

7. Fibonacci Retracement Strategy:

Fibonacci retracement levels are used to identify potential support and resistance levels based on the Fibonacci sequence. Traders use these levels alongside other technical indicators to identify potential entry and exit points.

8. VWAP (Volume Weighted Average Price) Strategy:

VWAP is a trading indicator that calculates the average price based on both price and trading volume. Traders use VWAP to identify potential buy or sell signals, especially in high-volume trading periods.

9. Gap Trading:

Gap trading involves taking advantage of price gaps that occur when the market opens higher or lower than the previous day's close. Traders enter positions to profit from the gap being filled or to ride the continuation of the gap movement.

10. Pivot Reversal Strategy:

The pivot reversal strategy involves identifying pivot points and looking for price reversals around these levels. Traders enter positions when the price shows signs of reversing after reaching a pivot point.

Day trading strategies in Forex involve a wide range of approaches to capitalize on short-term price movements. Each strategy has its unique characteristics, and successful day trading requires a deep understanding of market dynamics, technical analysis, and risk management. As with any trading style, it's essential to practice, maintain discipline, and continuously adapt your strategies to changing market conditions. Remember that day trading involves higher trading frequency and requires a strong focus on executing trades effectively and efficiently.

4.2 Swing Trading Strategies

Swing trading is a trading style that involves holding positions for several days to weeks, taking advantage of short- to medium-term price swings within a larger market trend. Swing traders aim to capture price movements between support and resistance levels or during corrective phases within a trend. Here are some common swing trading strategies used by Forex traders:

1. Trend Following:

Swing traders using the trend-following strategy identify and trade in the direction of the dominant market trend. They enter positions when the price retraces or pulls back within the trend, aiming to catch the continuation of the trend's momentum. Technical indicators like moving averages, MACD, and ADX are commonly used to identify trends and potential entry points.

2. Breakout Trading:

Breakout trading in swing trading involves entering positions when the price breaks above or below key support or resistance levels. Swing traders look for strong breakouts that may indicate the start of a new trend or a significant price movement. Volume and price action analysis are often used to confirm breakouts.

3. Support and Resistance Trading:

Swing traders using support and resistance trading look for key levels where the price has historically found support or encountered resistance. They enter positions when the price bounces off support or breaks through resistance, expecting the price to continue in the direction of the breakout.

4. Fibonacci Retracement Strategy:

Fibonacci retracement levels are used in swing trading to identify potential reversal points within a trend. Swing traders look for potential entry points near Fibonacci retracement levels, expecting the price to resume its original trend after a correction.

5. Moving Average Crossovers:

Moving average crossovers involve using two or more moving averages with different periods. Swing traders enter positions when a shorter-term moving average crosses above a longer-term moving average (golden cross) or crosses below (death cross), signaling potential trend changes.

6. Bullish and Bearish Engulfing Patterns:

Swing traders look for bullish engulfing patterns (a bullish candle fully engulfs the previous bearish candle) at support levels and bearish engulfing patterns (a bearish candle fully engulfs the previous bullish candle) at resistance levels as potential entry signals.

7. Moving Average Bounce:

Swing traders using the moving average bounce strategy enter positions when the price pulls back to a specific moving average and then resume its upward or downward movement. Moving averages act as dynamic support and resistance levels in this strategy.

8. RSI Divergence Strategy:

Swing traders use the Relative Strength Index (RSI) to identify potential trend reversals. They look for bullish divergence (higher lows in price but lower lows in RSI) as a potential buy signal and bearish divergence (lower highs in price but higher highs in RSI) as a potential sell signal.

9. Multiple Time Frame Analysis:

Swing traders often use multiple time frame analyses to identify trends in higher time frames and find entry and exit points in lower time frames. This approach helps traders align their trades with the broader market trend.

10. Bollinger Bands Strategy:

Swing traders use Bollinger Bands to identify potential price breakouts and reversals. They enter positions when the price breaks above the upper Bollinger Band (for a potential breakout) or below the lower Bollinger Band (for a potential reversal).

Swing trading strategies in Forex focus on capturing short- to medium-term price movements within the context of a larger market trend. Traders using these strategies aim to enter positions at strategic points, such as trend retracements, breakouts, or support and resistance levels. It's essential to use technical indicators and analysis techniques to confirm entry and exit points and apply sound risk management principles to manage trades effectively. Swing trading requires patience and discipline to hold positions for a few days to weeks, making it suitable for traders who prefer a less frequent trading approach than day trading.

4.3 Carry Trading Strategies

Carry trading is a popular Forex trading strategy that involves taking advantage of interest rate differentials between currency pairs. Traders aim to profit from the difference in interest rates by buying currencies with higher interest rates and selling currencies with lower interest rates. Carry trading is typically a longer-term strategy and may involve holding positions for weeks or even months. Here are some common carry trading strategies used by Forex traders:

1. **Currency Pair Selection:**

Carry traders carefully select currency pairs with significant interest rate differentials. They typically look for pairs where the base currency has a higher interest rate than the quote currency. For example, a common carry trade involves buying a currency with a higher interest rate, such as the New Zealand Dollar (NZD) or Australian Dollar (AUD), and selling a currency with a lower interest rate, such as the Japanese Yen (JPY) or Swiss Franc (CHF).

2. **Long-Term Holding:**

Carry trading involves holding positions for an extended period to benefit from the accrual of interest rate differentials. Traders may hold these positions for weeks or months to maximize potential returns from interest payments.

3. Risk Management:

Carry traders implement robust risk management strategies to protect their capital. They are aware that exchange rates can be volatile, which may affect the overall profitability of the trade. Implementing stop-loss orders and position sizing based on risk tolerance is essential to manage potential losses.

4. Consideration of Central Bank Policies:

Carry traders keep a close eye on central bank policies and interest rate decisions. Changes in interest rates can impact the interest rate differential and affect the attractiveness of the carry trade.

5. Diversification:

To spread risk, carry traders often diversify their portfolios by holding multiple carry trades across different currency pairs. This approach helps mitigate the impact of adverse movements in any single currency pair.

6. Roll-over Timing:

Carry traders pay attention to the timing of roll-over or swap rates, as these rates can vary depending on the broker and the currency pair. Some traders may strategically enter or exit positions just before the daily rollover to maximize or minimize the impact of swap rates.

7.   Economic Calendar Events:

Carry traders stay informed about major economic events that may impact interest rates or exchange rates. Economic indicators, central bank meetings, and geopolitical developments can affect currency valuations and should be considered in carrying trading strategies.

8.   Monitoring Currency Market Conditions:

Carry traders monitor the currency market regularly to identify potential changes in interest rate differentials or currency pair trends. They remain flexible and may adjust their positions based on changing market conditions.

9.   Calculating Carry Trade Potential:

Carry traders calculate the potential gains from the interest rate differentials and compare them to any potential capital appreciation or depreciation in the currency pair. This analysis helps in making informed trading decisions.

10. Fundamental Analysis:

Fundamental analysis is essential in carry trading to assess the overall economic health and monetary policies of the countries whose currencies are being traded. Positive economic outlooks and higher interest rate expectations may enhance the appeal of carry trades.

Carry trading is a popular Forex strategy that takes advantage of interest rate differentials between currency pairs. By holding positions for a more extended period, traders aim to profit from the accrual of interest rate payments. Successful carry trading involves selecting currency pairs with favorable interest rate differentials, implementing effective risk management, and staying informed about economic events and central bank policies. As with any trading strategy, careful analysis and prudent risk management are essential for long-term success in carry trading.

4.4 Breakout Trading Strategies

Breakout trading is a popular Forex trading strategy that involves identifying and trading the price movements that occur when the price breaks above or below key support or resistance levels. Breakouts often indicate potential trend reversals or the continuation of existing trends, and traders aim to profit from the resulting price momentum. Here are some common breakout trading strategies used by Forex traders:

1. Support and Resistance Breakouts:

Traders using this strategy look for key support levels where the price has historically bounced higher and resistance levels where the price has historically reversed lower. When the price breaks above a resistance level or below a support level, traders enter positions in the direction of the breakout.

2. Chart Pattern Breakouts:

Breakout traders also look for specific chart patterns that can signal potential breakouts. Common chart patterns include triangles, rectangles, head and shoulders, and double tops/bottoms. Traders enter positions when the price breaks out of the pattern, confirming the potential continuation or reversal of the trend.

3. Volatility Breakouts:

Volatility breakout strategies involve entering positions when the price experiences a sudden increase in volatility. Traders use indicators like Bollinger Bands, Average True Range (ATR), or Donchian Channels to identify periods of low volatility, which can precede significant price movements.

4. Fibonacci Breakouts:

Fibonacci retracement and extension levels are used to identify potential support and resistance levels. Traders look for breakouts above or below these levels, signaling potential trend continuation or reversal.

5. Breakout and Retest:

Traders using the breakout and retest strategy wait for a breakout to occur and then enter positions after the price retraces back to the breakout level, confirming the validity of the breakout. This approach helps traders avoid false breakouts.

6. News-Driven Breakouts:

Breakouts can occur as a result of significant economic news or geopolitical events. Traders monitor economic calendars and news announcements to enter positions quickly after news-driven breakouts.

7. Moving Average Breakouts:

Moving averages act as dynamic support and resistance levels. Traders look for breakouts above or below moving averages, such as the 50-day or 200-day moving averages, as potential entry signals.

8. Trendline Breakouts:

Traders draw trendlines to connect higher lows in an uptrend or lower highs in a downtrend. When the price breaks above or below the trendline, it can signal a potential trend continuation or reversal.

9. Breakouts with Volume Confirmation:

Volume can provide additional confirmation for breakouts. Traders look for breakouts accompanied by higher-than-average trading volume, which suggests stronger market participation and conviction.

10. Range Breakouts:

Traders identify currency pairs that have been trading within a defined range and enter positions when the price breaks out of the range. Range breakouts can lead to significant price movements.

Breakout trading strategies in Forex involve identifying key price levels or chart patterns where the price is likely to experience a significant movement. Traders enter positions when the price breaks above or below these levels, aiming to profit from the resulting price momentum. Successful breakout trading requires careful analysis, risk management, and discipline in executing trades. Traders should be cautious of false breakouts and use additional indicators or volume confirmation to increase the probability of successful breakout trades. As with any trading strategy, continuous learning and practice are essential for becoming proficient in breakout trading.

Chapter 5: Chart Patterns and Indicators

In this chapter, we will explore various chart patterns and technical indicators used by Forex traders to analyze market trends, identify potential entry and exit points, and make informed trading decisions. Chart patterns and indicators provide valuable insights into market behavior, helping traders to spot opportunities and manage risk effectively. Let's delve into some commonly used chart patterns and indicators in Forex trading:

1. **Chart Patterns:**

Chart patterns are recurring formations on price charts that can signal potential trend reversals or continuations. Some popular chart patterns include:

- Head and Shoulders: A pattern that resembles a head with two shoulders, signaling a potential trend reversal from bullish to bearish (inverse head and shoulders for a bullish reversal).
- Double Tops and Bottoms: A pattern with two peaks (double top) or two troughs (double bottom) that suggests a potential trend reversal.
- Triangles: Triangles form when the price consolidates, indicating a potential breakout in the future. Types include ascending, descending, and symmetrical triangles.
- Flags and Pennants: These patterns form after sharp price movements and indicate a continuation of the existing trend.
- Cup and Handle: A bullish continuation pattern that resembles a cup with a handle, signaling potential upward price movement.

2.   Moving Averages (MA):

Moving averages are trend-following indicators that smooth out price data over a specific period. The most common types are the Simple Moving Average (SMA) and the Exponential Moving Average (EMA). Traders use moving averages to identify trends, potential support and resistance levels, and crossovers for entry and exit signals.

3.   Relative Strength Index (RSI):

The RSI is a momentum oscillator that measures the speed and change of price movements. It ranges from 0 to 100 and indicates overbought conditions (above 70) and oversold conditions (below 30). Traders use RSI to spot potential trend reversals and divergences between price and oscillator.

4.   Moving Average Convergence Divergence (MACD):

The MACD is a versatile indicator that combines moving averages to identify trend direction and momentum. Traders use MACD crossovers and histogram values to generate buy and sell signals.

5.   Bollinger Bands:

Bollinger Bands consist of a central moving average and two standard deviation bands. They dynamically adjust to market volatility, contracting during low volatility and expanding during high volatility.

Traders use Bollinger Bands to identify overbought and oversold conditions and potential price breakouts.

6.   Fibonacci Retracement and Extension Levels:

Fibonacci levels are derived from the Fibonacci sequence and are used to identify potential support and resistance levels. Traders use these levels alongside other technical tools to find potential entry and exit points.

7.   Ichimoku Cloud:

The Ichimoku Cloud is a comprehensive indicator that provides information about trend direction, support and resistance levels, and potential future price movements. Traders use the cloud, conversion line, and baseline for signals.

8.   Parabolic SAR (Stop and Reverse):

The Parabolic SAR is used to identify potential trend reversals. It appears as dots above or below the price chart, indicating a potential shift in trend direction.

9.   Average True Range (ATR):

ATR measures market volatility by calculating the average range between high and low prices over a specific period. Traders use ATR to set stop-loss levels and position sizing based on market volatility.

10. Stochastic Oscillator:

The Stochastic Oscillator compares a security's closing price to its price range over a specific period. It indicates overbought and oversold conditions, helping traders identify potential reversals.

Chart patterns and technical indicators are invaluable tools for Forex traders to analyze market trends, identify potential trading opportunities, and make informed decisions. By understanding and combining these patterns and indicators, traders can enhance their ability to navigate the dynamic and competitive Forex market. It is essential to use chart patterns and indicators in conjunction with proper risk management and other fundamental and technical analysis methods for a comprehensive trading approach. Continual learning and practice are essential for traders to become proficient in using chart patterns and indicators effectively to achieve consistent profits in Forex trading.

5.1 Identifying Chart Patterns

Identifying chart patterns is an important skill for Forex traders as it helps them spot potential trend reversals or continuations, providing valuable insights for making trading decisions. Chart patterns are visual formations that occur on price charts and can offer clues about the future price direction. Here are some common chart patterns and tips for identifying them:

1. **Head and Shoulders:**

The head and shoulders pattern consists of three peaks, with the middle peak (the head) being higher than the other two (the shoulders). This pattern signals a potential trend reversal from bullish to bearish. Traders identify this pattern when the price forms three distinct peaks, and the trendline connecting the two shoulders acts as the neckline.

2. **Double Tops and Bottoms:**

Double tops and bottoms are reversal patterns. A double top pattern forms when the price reaches a peak, retraces, and then tests the previous peak without breaking higher. A double bottom pattern occurs when the price reaches a trough, retraces, and then tests the previous trough without breaking lower. These patterns indicate potential trend reversals.

3. **Triangles:**

Triangles are consolidation patterns characterized by converging trendlines. Three common types of triangles are:

- Ascending Triangle: A flat top trendline and an upward-sloping bottom trendline. It suggests a potential bullish breakout.
- Descending Triangle: A flat bottom trendline and a downward-sloping top trendline. It suggests a potential bearish breakout.

- Symmetrical Triangle: Both the top and bottom trendlines converge. The direction of the breakout is not predetermined.

4. Flags and Pennants:

Flags and pennants are continuation patterns that occur after strong price movements. A flag resembles a rectangular shape, while a pennant looks like a small symmetrical triangle. Both patterns signal a potential continuation of the existing trend after a brief consolidation.

5. Cup and Handle:

The cup and handle pattern is a bullish continuation pattern. It looks like a cup followed by a smaller handle. The price forms the cup by reaching a high and then pulling back. It then consolidates to form the handle before breaking out to the upside.

6. Wedges:

Wedges are patterns with both trendlines converging. Two common types are:

- Rising Wedge: Both the upper and lower trendlines are upward-sloping, suggesting a potential bearish reversal.
- Falling Wedge: Both the upper and lower trendlines are downward-sloping, indicating a potential bullish reversal.

7. Rectangle:

A rectangle is a horizontal trading range with both support and resistance levels almost parallel. Traders look for potential breakouts in either direction after the price consolidates within the rectangle.

8. Rounded Bottom (Saucer) and Top:

Rounded bottoms resemble a gentle upward curve, signaling a potential bullish reversal. Rounded tops have a gentle downward curve, indicating a potential bearish reversal.

9. Gaps:

Gaps occur when the price opens significantly higher or lower than the previous day's close. Common types are breakaway gaps, continuation gaps, and exhaustion gaps. Gaps can signal potential changes in market sentiment.

10. Candlestick Patterns:

Candlestick patterns, such as doji, engulfing patterns, hammers, and shooting stars, provide valuable information about market sentiment and potential trend reversals.

Identifying chart patterns is a skill that can significantly enhance a trader's ability to read market trends and make informed trading decisions. By recognizing these patterns, traders can spot potential entry and exit points and apply appropriate risk management strategies. It is essential to combine chart patterns with other technical and fundamental analysis tools for a comprehensive approach to Forex trading. Regular practice and continuous learning are essential for traders to become proficient in identifying chart patterns effectively and using them to navigate the dynamic Forex market.

5.2 Understanding Technical Indicators

Understanding technical indicators is crucial for Forex traders as they provide valuable insights into market trends, momentum, volatility, and potential entry and exit points. Technical indicators are mathematical calculations based on historical price and volume data. Traders use them to analyze past price behavior and predict future price movements. Here are some common technical indicators and their functions:

1. **Moving Averages (MA):**

Moving averages smooth out price data over a specific period, helping traders identify trends and potential support and resistance levels. The Simple Moving Average (SMA) calculates the average price over a defined number of periods, while the Exponential Moving Average (EMA) gives more weight to recent prices, making it more responsive to current market conditions.

2. **Relative Strength Index (RSI):**

The RSI is a momentum oscillator that measures the speed and change of price movements. It oscillates between 0 and 100 and indicates overbought conditions (above 70) and oversold conditions (below 30). Traders use the RSI to spot potential trend reversals and divergences between price and the indicator.

3. Moving Average Convergence Divergence (MACD):

The MACD is a versatile indicator that combines moving averages to identify trend direction and momentum. It consists of two lines: the MACD line (the difference between two moving averages) and the signal line (EMA of the MACD line). Traders use MACD crossovers and histogram values to generate buy and sell signals.

4. Bollinger Bands:

Bollinger Bands consist of a central moving average (typically the 20-period SMA) and two standard deviation bands. The bands expand during high volatility and contract during low volatility. Traders use Bollinger Bands to identify overbought and oversold conditions and potential price breakouts.

5. Fibonacci Retracement and Extension Levels:

Fibonacci levels are derived from the Fibonacci sequence and are used to identify potential support and resistance levels. Traders use these levels alongside other technical tools to find potential entry and exit points.

6. Ichimoku Cloud:

The Ichimoku Cloud is a comprehensive indicator that provides information about trend direction, support and resistance levels, and potential future price movements. It consists of five lines: Tenkan-sen, Kijun-sen, Senkou Span A, Senkou Span B, and Chikou Span. Traders use the cloud, conversion line, and baseline for signals.

7. Parabolic SAR (Stop and Reverse):

The Parabolic SAR is used to identify potential trend reversals. It appears as dots above or below the price chart, indicating a potential shift in trend direction.

8. Average True Range (ATR):

ATR measures market volatility by calculating the average range between high and low prices over a specific period. Traders use ATR to set stop-loss levels and position sizing based on market volatility.

9. Stochastic Oscillator:

The Stochastic Oscillator compares a security's closing price to its price range over a specific period. It indicates overbought and oversold conditions, helping traders identify potential reversals.

10. Volume Indicators:

Volume indicators, such as On-Balance-Volume (OBV) and Volume Weighted Average Price (VWAP), analyze trading volume to gauge market strength and confirm price trends.

Technical indicators play a vital role in Forex trading by providing valuable insights into market behavior. Traders use these indicators to identify trends, potential reversals, and entry and exit points. Understanding the functions and interpretations of technical indicators is essential for making informed trading decisions and developing effective trading strategies. As with any analysis tool, it's essential to use technical indicators in conjunction with other forms of analysis and apply proper risk management to achieve consistent profits in Forex trading. Continuous learning and practice are essential for traders to become proficient in using technical indicators effectively and staying ahead in the ever-changing Forex market.

5.3 Using Moving Averages

Moving averages (MA) are versatile and widely used technical indicators in Forex trading. They help traders identify trends, smooth out price fluctuations, and generate potential entry and exit signals. Here are some common ways traders use moving averages in their trading strategies:

1. Identifying Trends:

One of the primary uses of moving averages is to identify market trends. Traders analyze the slope and positioning of moving averages to determine if the market is in an uptrend, downtrend, or range. A rising moving average indicates an uptrend, while a falling moving average suggests a downtrend. When the market is ranging, the moving averages may move sideways.

2. Moving Average Crossovers:

Traders use moving average crossovers to generate entry and exit signals. A popular crossover strategy involves using two moving averages of different periods, such as the 50-period and 200-period moving averages. When the shorter-term moving average crosses above the longer-term moving average (golden cross), it generates a buy signal. Conversely, when the shorter-term moving average crosses below the longer-term moving average (death cross), it generates a sell signal.

3. Support and Resistance Levels:

Moving averages act as dynamic support and resistance levels. In an uptrend, the moving average may act as support, and in a downtrend, it may act as resistance. Traders watch for price reactions around moving averages to make trading decisions.

4. Moving Average Bounce and Break:

Traders use moving averages to identify potential entry and exit points. In a moving average bounce strategy, traders enter long positions when the price bounces off the moving average in an uptrend. In a moving average break strategy, traders enter long positions when the price breaks above the moving average, confirming a potential trend continuation.

5. Multiple Moving Averages:

Using multiple moving averages of different periods helps traders gain more insights into market trends and potential crossovers. For example, traders might use the 20-period, 50-period, and 200-period moving averages to assess short-term, medium-term, and long-term trends, respectively.

6. Moving Average Envelopes:

Moving average envelopes are lines drawn above and below a moving average at a specific percentage distance. They help traders identify potential overbought and oversold conditions. When the price moves above the upper envelope, it may indicate overbought conditions, and when it moves below the lower envelope, it may indicate oversold conditions.

7. Moving Average as a Trailing Stop:

Traders can use moving averages as a trailing stop-loss level. As the price moves in their favor, they adjust the stop-loss level to the moving average to protect profits while allowing the trade to stay open as long as the trend persists.

8. Moving Average Divergence:

Traders look for divergences between the moving average and the price. A divergence occurs when the price forms higher highs or lower lows, but the moving average fails to confirm the same pattern. This can signal a potential trend reversal.

Moving averages are valuable tools in Forex trading that help traders identify trends, generate entry and exit signals, and manage risk effectively. Traders can use single or multiple moving averages in various combinations, depending on their trading style and objectives. While moving averages are versatile, it is essential to use them in conjunction with other technical indicators and analysis methods for a comprehensive approach to trading. Continual learning and practice are key to mastering the effective use of moving averages in the dynamic and competitive Forex market.

5.4 RSI, MACD, and Stochastic Oscillator

RSI (Relative Strength Index), MACD (Moving Average Convergence Divergence), and Stochastic Oscillator are three popular technical indicators used by Forex traders to analyze market trends, momentum, and potential entry and exit points. Each indicator has unique characteristics and provides valuable insights into the price behavior of currency pairs. Let's take a closer look at each of these indicators:

1. Relative Strength Index (RSI):

The RSI is a momentum oscillator that measures the speed and change of price movements. It ranges from 0 to 100 and indicates overbought conditions (RSI above 70) and oversold conditions (RSI below 30). The RSI compares the magnitude of recent gains to recent losses and generates values that can be interpreted as the strength of a trend.

Interpretation:

- RSI above 70: Indicates overbought conditions, suggesting that the currency pair may be due for a downward correction or reversal.
- RSI below 30: Indicates oversold conditions, suggesting that the currency pair may be due for an upward correction or reversal.
- Bullish Divergence: This occurs when the price forms lower lows, but the RSI forms higher lows, indicating a potential bullish reversal.

- Bearish Divergence: This occurs when the price forms higher highs, but the RSI forms lower highs, indicating a potential bearish reversal.

2. Moving Average Convergence Divergence (MACD):

The MACD is a versatile indicator that combines moving averages to identify trend direction and momentum. It consists of two lines:

- MACD Line: The difference between two moving averages (usually the 12-period EMA and the 26-period EMA).
- Signal Line: The 9-period EMA of the MACD line.

Interpretation:

- MACD Line above Signal Line: Indicates a bullish signal, suggesting that the price is likely to continue upward.
- MACD Line below Signal Line: Indicates a bearish signal, suggesting that the price is likely to continue downward.
- MACD Histogram: The difference between the MACD line and the signal line. Positive histogram bars indicate bullish momentum, while negative bars indicate bearish momentum.

3. Stochastic Oscillator:

The Stochastic Oscillator compares a security's closing price to its price range over a specific period. It oscillates between 0 and 100 and helps identify overbought and oversold conditions.

Interpretation:

- Stochastic above 80: Indicates overbought conditions, suggesting that the currency pair may be due for a downward correction or reversal.
- Stochastic below 20: Indicates oversold conditions, suggesting that the currency pair may be due for an upward correction or reversal.
- Bullish Signal: Occurs when the %K line crosses above the %D line and both lines are below 80, indicating potential upward momentum.
- Bearish Signal: Occurs when the %K line crosses below the %D line and both lines are above 20, indicating potential downward momentum.

RSI, MACD, and Stochastic Oscillator are popular technical indicators used by Forex traders to analyze market trends, identify potential reversals, and generate entry and exit signals. Traders often use these indicators in conjunction with other technical tools and analysis methods to form a comprehensive trading strategy. It's important to remember that no single indicator should be used in isolation, and prudent risk management practices should always be employed when using these indicators to make trading decisions. Continuous learning and practice are essential for traders to become proficient in utilizing RSI, MACD, and Stochastic Oscillator effectively in the dynamic and competitive Forex market.

Chapter 6: Advanced Forex Trading Techniques

In this chapter, we will explore advanced Forex trading techniques that go beyond the basics and require a deeper understanding of market dynamics and trading strategies. These advanced techniques are utilized by experienced traders to gain a competitive edge and enhance their trading performance. Let's delve into some of these advanced techniques:

1. Advanced Risk Management:

Risk management is a critical aspect of successful Forex trading. Advanced traders implement sophisticated risk management techniques to protect their capital and minimize losses. This may involve using techniques such as position sizing based on risk tolerance, diversifying the portfolio across various currency pairs and asset classes, and utilizing trailing stops to protect profits while allowing trades to run.

2. Pyramiding:

Pyramiding is a technique where traders add to their winning positions as the trade goes in their favor. Instead of taking a full position at once, advanced traders enter a small position initially and then add to it as the trade becomes more profitable. This technique allows traders to maximize profits during strong trends while managing risk effectively.

3. Mean Reversion Trading:

Mean reversion trading is a strategy based on the idea that prices tend to revert to their average over time. Advanced traders identify overbought and oversold conditions using technical indicators or statistical analysis and take positions with the expectation that prices will return to their average value.

4. High-Frequency Trading (HFT):

High-frequency trading is a sophisticated technique that involves using powerful algorithms and computer programs to execute a large number of trades in a fraction of a second. HFT is based on exploiting small price discrepancies and is typically used by institutional traders and hedge funds.

5. Algorithmic Trading:

Algorithmic trading, also known as algo-trading, is the use of pre-defined rules and algorithms to automate trading decisions. Advanced traders develop their custom algorithms or use existing ones to execute trades based on various technical indicators, news events, or market patterns.

6. Seasonality Trading:

Seasonality trading involves identifying recurring patterns in the Forex market based on the time of the year or certain events. Advanced traders analyze historical data to recognize these seasonal patterns and use them as part of their trading strategy.

7. Arbitrage Trading:

Arbitrage trading seeks to profit from price discrepancies of the same currency pair or related instruments in different markets. Advanced traders identify price differences and execute trades to exploit these discrepancies for risk-free profit.

8. Order Flow Trading:

Order flow trading involves analyzing the volume and order flow data to gain insights into market sentiment and potential price movements. Advanced traders study order book data and market depth to make informed trading decisions.

9. Intermarket Analysis:

Intermarket analysis involves studying the relationships between different financial markets, such as Forex, stocks, commodities, and bonds. Advanced traders use this analysis to gain a broader understanding of market trends and correlations, which can aid in making more accurate predictions.

10. Elliott Wave Theory:

Elliott Wave Theory is a complex technical analysis approach that identifies recurring patterns in market price movements. Advanced traders use this theory to forecast potential market trends and reversals based on wave patterns.

Advanced Forex trading techniques require a higher level of expertise, experience, and knowledge of the financial markets. These techniques are utilized by seasoned traders to gain an edge in the competitive world of Forex trading. While some techniques, such as high-frequency trading and algorithmic trading, are more suitable for institutional traders, others like advanced risk management and Intermarket analysis can benefit retail traders as well. It's essential to remember that advanced techniques come with higher risks and complexities, so continuous learning, thorough research, and disciplined execution are crucial for successful implementation. As traders progress in their journey, they may integrate these advanced techniques into their trading strategies to achieve consistent profitability and long-term success in the Forex market.

6.1 Fibonacci Retracement and Extensions

Fibonacci retracement and extensions are powerful technical analysis tools used by Forex traders to identify potential support and resistance levels, as well as to forecast potential price targets. These tools are based on the Fibonacci sequence, a mathematical sequence in which each number is the sum of the two preceding ones. The key Fibonacci retracement levels are 23.6%, 38.2%, 50%, 61.8%, and 78.6%, while the common extension levels are 127.2%, 161.8%, 261.8%, and 423.6%. Here's how traders use Fibonacci retracement and extensions:

1. Fibonacci Retracement:

Fibonacci retracement levels are drawn on a price chart to identify potential support and resistance levels during a market retracement. The retracement levels help traders determine the extent to which the price is likely to pull back against the prevailing trend before potentially continuing in the original direction. Here's how to use Fibonacci retracement:

- Identify the Trend: First, determine the direction of the prevailing trend. Fibonacci retracement is most effective when used in trending markets.
- Draw the Retracement Levels: Select the swing high and swing low points on the chart. The swing high is the peak point of the uptrend, and the swing low is the bottom point of the downtrend. Then, draw the Fibonacci retracement levels from the swing high to the swing low.
- Analyze Potential Support and Resistance: The Fibonacci retracement levels act as potential support levels during an uptrend and resistance levels during a downtrend. Traders look for price reactions, such as bounces or reversals, around these levels to identify potential entry and exit points.

2. Fibonacci Extensions:

Fibonacci extensions are used to identify potential price targets beyond the initial trend. These levels help traders anticipate where the price may move after a significant trend or breakout has occurred. Here's how to use Fibonacci extensions:

- Identify the Trend: As with Fibonacci retracement, start by identifying the direction of the prevailing trend.
- Draw the Extension Levels: Select the swing high and swing low points on the chart. Then, draw the Fibonacci extension levels from the swing low to the swing high.
- Project Potential Price Targets: The Fibonacci extension levels act as potential price targets for the continuation of the trend. Traders use these levels to identify potential profit-taking or exit points.

Fibonacci retracement and extensions are valuable tools in Forex trading that help traders identify potential support and resistance levels and forecast potential price targets. By understanding and applying these levels, traders can enhance their ability to make informed trading decisions. As with any technical analysis tool, it is essential to use Fibonacci retracement and extensions in conjunction with other technical indicators and analysis methods for a comprehensive approach to trading. Continual learning and practice are key to mastering the effective use of Fibonacci retracement and extensions in the dynamic and competitive Forex market.

6.2 Elliot Wave Theory

Elliott Wave Theory is a complex and widely used technical analysis approach that aims to identify recurring patterns in market price movements. It was developed by Ralph Nelson Elliott in the 1930s and is based on the principle that market prices move in recognizable wave patterns driven by investor psychology. The theory suggests that markets move in a series of impulsive waves (trending moves) and corrective waves (counter-trend moves). Understanding Elliott Wave Theory can help Forex traders anticipate potential market trends and reversals. Here are the key principles of Elliott Wave Theory:

1. Five-Wave Impulse Pattern:

In an uptrend, the theory suggests that prices advance in a series of five upward-moving waves (designated as 1, 2, 3, 4, and 5). Waves 1, 3, and 5 are impulsive waves, and they move in the direction of the prevailing trend. Waves 2 and 4 are corrective waves, which move against the trend.

2. Three-Wave Corrective Pattern:

Following the completion of the five-wave impulse pattern, a three-wave corrective pattern (designated as A, B, and C) follows. Corrective waves aim to retrace a portion of the previous impulse waves.

3. Wave Degree and Hierarchy:

Elliott Wave Theory introduces the concept of wave degrees to describe the different scales of waves. The smallest wave is referred to as a Subminuette, followed by Minuette, Minor, Intermediate, Primary, Cycle, Supercycle, and Grand Supercycle waves. Each higher-degree wave contains a pattern of lower-degree waves within it.

4. Fibonacci Ratio:

Elliott Wave Theory often incorporates Fibonacci ratios in measuring the extent of wave movements. Common ratios used include 0.382, 0.500, 0.618, 1.618, and others.

5. Wave Count and Alternation:

Properly identifying and counting waves is crucial in Elliott Wave analysis. Traders look for alternation between different types of waves (e.g., wave 2 might be a simple correction, while wave 4 might be more complex) to validate the wave count.

6. Channeling:

Elliott Wave analysts use trend channels and trendlines to provide support and resistance levels for waves, helping to identify potential entry and exit points.

7. Application in Forex Trading:

Elliott Wave Theory is a complex analysis method that requires significant skill and experience to apply effectively. Forex traders use Elliott Wave analysis to identify potential trend reversals, confirm price targets, and gain insights into market sentiment. Traders often combine Elliott Wave analysis with other technical indicators and fundamental analysis to make informed trading decisions.

Elliott Wave Theory is a sophisticated and widely followed technical analysis method used by Forex traders to identify patterns and predict potential market trends and reversals. It offers valuable insights into market psychology and price movements, but it requires expertise and discipline to apply successfully. Traders should use caution and practice when incorporating Elliott Wave analysis into their trading strategies, and continuous learning is essential to becoming proficient in this complex analysis approach.

6.3 Price Action Trading

Price action trading is a popular and widely used trading strategy that relies on analyzing raw price movements on a chart without the use of technical indicators or other external factors. Price action traders believe that all the necessary information to make trading decisions is reflected in the price itself and that understanding price patterns and market behavior can lead to profitable trading opportunities. Here are the key principles and concepts of price action trading:

1. Candlestick Patterns:

Candlestick patterns are a crucial element of price action trading. Traders analyze the shapes and formations of candlesticks to identify potential market reversals, continuations, and indecision points. Common candlestick patterns include doji, engulfing patterns, hammers, shooting stars, and more.

2. Support and Resistance Levels:

Price action traders pay close attention to support and resistance levels, which are areas on the chart where the price tends to reverse or stall. These levels can be identified based on previous price highs and lows and act as potential entry and exit points for trades.

3. Trend Analysis:

Price action traders analyze the structure of trends and trendlines to determine the prevailing market direction. They look for higher highs and higher lows in an uptrend and lower highs and lower lows in a downtrend. Understanding the trend helps traders align their trades with the overall market sentiment.

4. Price Action Patterns:

Price action traders look for specific price patterns, such as double tops and bottoms, head and shoulders, triangles, flags, and pennants, to identify potential trading opportunities. These patterns can indicate the continuation or reversal of a trend.

5. Candlestick Reversal Patterns:

Price action traders focus on candlestick reversal patterns, such as pin bars, hammers, and shooting stars that suggest a potential change in market sentiment. These patterns often occur at key support and resistance levels, adding to their significance.

6. Engulfing Patterns:

Engulfing patterns occur when one candlestick completely engulfs the previous one. Bullish engulfing patterns indicate potential upward reversals, while bearish engulfing patterns suggest potential downward reversals.

7. Price Action Trading Strategies:

Price action traders use various trading strategies, such as breakout trading, trend trading, and range trading. Each strategy involves different approaches to identifying potential entry and exit points based on price patterns and market conditions.

8. Risk Management:

Like any trading approach, risk management is essential in price action trading. Traders use stop-loss orders and position-sizing techniques to protect their capital and manage risk effectively.

Price action trading is a straightforward yet powerful approach to Forex trading that relies on analyzing raw price movements on a chart to identify trading opportunities. Traders who adopt this strategy aim to gain a deep understanding of market behavior and sentiment without the need for complex technical indicators. By focusing on price patterns, support and resistance levels, and trend analysis, price action traders can make well-informed trading decisions and achieve consistent profitability in the dynamic and competitive Forex market. Continuous learning, practice, and discipline are crucial for traders to become proficient in price action trading and utilize it effectively in their trading strategies.

6.4 Trading Divergences

Trading divergences is a popular and effective strategy used by Forex traders to identify potential trend reversals and market turning points. Divergence occurs when the price of a currency pair moves in a different direction than a technical indicator, indicating a potential shift in market sentiment. Traders use divergences to make informed trading decisions and spot potential entry and exit points. There are two main types of divergences: bullish divergence and bearish divergence.

1. Bullish Divergence:

A bullish divergence occurs when the price forms lower lows, but the indicator (such as the Relative Strength Index - RSI or Moving Average Convergence Divergence - MACD) forms higher lows. This discrepancy suggests that the downward momentum in the price is weakening, and a potential bullish reversal may be imminent. It indicates that buyers might be stepping in, creating a possible opportunity for long positions.

2. Bearish Divergence:

A bearish divergence occurs when the price forms higher highs, but the indicator forms lower highs. This indicates that the upward momentum in the price is weakening, and a potential bearish reversal may be on the horizon. It suggests that sellers might be gaining strength, creating a potential opportunity for short positions.

How to Trade Divergences:

Trading divergences involve the following steps:

- Identify the Trend: Determine the prevailing trend in the market. Divergences are most effective when they occur within the context of an established trend.
- Select the Indicator: Choose a suitable technical indicator, such as RSI, MACD, or Stochastic Oscillator, that can effectively show divergences.
- Spot Divergence: Look for divergences between the price and the chosen indicator. Pay attention to lower lows and higher lows in the price compared to the indicator, or higher highs and lower highs in the price compared to the indicator.
- Confirm the Divergence: Confirm the presence of the divergence with multiple time frames or other indicators. It helps to ensure the reliability of the divergence signal.
- Entry and Exit Points: Once the divergence is confirmed, traders can plan their entry and exit points. For bullish divergence, they may consider going long, and for bearish divergence, they may consider going short.

- Risk Management: Implement proper risk management techniques, such as setting stop-loss orders to limit potential losses if the trade doesn't go as expected.
- Monitor the Trade: Keep a close eye on the trade and manage it accordingly as the price continues to evolve.

Trading divergences is a valuable technique that helps Forex traders identify potential trend reversals and turning points in the market. By spotting discrepancies between price movements and technical indicators, traders can gain insights into market sentiment and make informed trading decisions. However, as with any trading strategy, it's essential to combine divergences with other technical and fundamental analysis tools and apply proper risk management practices to achieve consistent profits in Forex trading. Continuous learning, practice, and experience are key to mastering the art of trading divergences effectively.

Chapter 7: Risk Management and Psychology

In this chapter, we will explore two crucial aspects of successful Forex trading: risk management and psychology. Both risk management and psychology play integral roles in determining a trader's long-term success and profitability. Let's delve into each of these aspects:

Risk Management

1. Importance of Risk Management:

Effective risk management is the foundation of a successful trading career. It involves strategies and techniques to protect capital and minimize losses while maximizing potential profits. Traders must understand that every trade involves inherent risks, and controlling those risks is essential for survival in the market.

2. Position Sizing:

Position sizing refers to determining the appropriate amount of capital to allocate to each trade. Traders should avoid risking a substantial portion of their capital on a single trade and instead use position sizing techniques to limit each trade's risk to a small percentage of their trading capital.

3. Setting Stop-Loss Orders:

Stop-loss orders are pre-defined price levels at which a trade will be automatically closed to limit potential losses. Placing stop-loss orders ensures that a trader exits a losing trade before it incurs significant damage to their account.

4. Using Take-Profit Orders:

Take-profit orders are pre-defined price levels at which a trade will be automatically closed to secure profits. Having a target for profit-taking ensures that traders lock in gains when the market moves in their favor.

5. Diversification:

Diversifying the trading portfolio across various currency pairs and assets can help spread risk and reduce exposure to any single market.

Trading Psychology

1. Emotions and Trading:

Controlling emotions is one of the most challenging aspects of Forex trading. Emotions like fear, greed, and overconfidence can lead to impulsive and irrational decisions. Successful traders maintain emotional discipline and adhere to their trading plans.

2. Patience and Discipline:

Patience is a virtue in Forex trading. Waiting for high-probability setups and not forcing trades can lead to more consistent and successful trading results. Discipline ensures that traders stick to their trading strategies and do not deviate based on emotions or market noise.

3. Dealing with Losses:

Losses are a natural part of trading. Successful traders accept losses as a learning opportunity and avoid chasing losses or revenge trading, which can lead to even more significant losses.

4. Building Confidence:

Building confidence in one's trading abilities comes from knowledge, experience, and having a well-tested trading plan. Confidence allows traders to execute trades without second-guessing themselves.

5. Continuous Learning:

Forex markets are dynamic, and continuous learning is essential for traders to stay updated with market trends and refine their trading strategies.

Risk management and psychology are essential components of successful Forex trading. By implementing effective risk management strategies, traders protect their capital and reduce the impact of losses. Managing emotions and maintaining discipline is crucial for making rational and informed trading decisions. Successful traders understand that trading is a journey of continuous learning and improvement. By mastering risk management and psychology, traders can enhance their chances of long-term success in the challenging and rewarding world of Forex trading.

7.1 The Psychology of Forex Trading

The psychology of Forex trading refers to the emotional and mental aspects that influence a trader's decision-making process in the Forex market. Understanding and managing the psychological factors that come into play during trading is crucial for achieving long-term success. Forex trading can be emotionally challenging, and emotions such as fear, greed, impatience, and overconfidence can significantly impact a trader's performance. Let's explore some key aspects of the psychology of Forex trading:

1. Emotions and Trading:

Emotions play a significant role in trading and can lead to impulsive decisions. Fear of losses may prevent traders from taking valid trading opportunities, while greed can lead to chasing high-risk trades. Emotions can cloud judgment and lead to emotional trading, which often results in poor trading outcomes.

2. Maintaining Emotional Discipline:

Emotional discipline is essential for successful trading. It involves sticking to a well-defined trading plan and executing trades based on pre-defined rules rather than emotional impulses. Maintaining emotional discipline helps traders avoid making rash decisions driven by fear or excitement.

3. Dealing with Losses:

Losses are an inevitable part of trading, and how traders deal with them is critical. Accepting losses as a natural part of the trading process, learning from them, and moving forward is essential. Traders should avoid revenge trading or attempting to recover losses quickly, as it can lead to more significant losses.

4. Managing Greed and Overconfidence:

Greed and overconfidence can lead to excessive risk-taking and neglecting risk management principles. Successful traders remain realistic about their abilities and avoid becoming overconfident in their trading strategies.

5. Patience and Discipline:

Patience is crucial in Forex trading. Waiting for high-probability trade setups and not forcing trades out of impatience leads to better trading results. Discipline ensures that traders adhere to their trading plans and do not deviate based on emotions or market noise.

6. Avoiding Information Overload:

The Forex market provides a vast amount of information, and traders may feel overwhelmed by continuous news and analysis. Managing information overload is essential to focus on relevant market factors and avoid making decisions based on noise.

7. Building Trading Confidence:

Confidence in trading comes from knowledge, experience, and a well-tested trading plan. Building trading confidence allows traders to execute trades without hesitation and stay committed to their strategies.

8. Continuous Learning and Adaptation:

Forex markets are dynamic and ever-changing. Traders need to embrace continuous learning and adapt their strategies to new market conditions to stay ahead in the market.

The psychology of Forex trading is a critical aspect of becoming a successful trader. Managing emotions, maintaining discipline, and dealing with losses is essential for effective decision-making. Traders must develop emotional resilience to cope with the ups and downs of the market and remain focused on their long-term trading goals. By understanding and mastering the psychological aspects of trading, traders can develop the mental fortitude needed to navigate the challenging and exciting world of Forex trading with confidence and consistency. Continuous self-awareness, improvement, and practice are key to enhancing the psychology of Forex trading and achieving long-term success.

7.2 Emotional Management

Emotional management, also known as emotional discipline or emotional intelligence, is a crucial aspect of successful Forex trading. It refers to the ability of traders to recognize, understand, and manage their emotions effectively during the trading process. Emotions play a significant role in trading decisions, and emotional management is essential for maintaining rationality, discipline, and consistency in trading. Here are some key points on emotional management in Forex trading:

1. Self-Awareness:

The first step in emotional management is self-awareness. Traders should recognize and acknowledge their emotions as they arise during trading. Being aware of emotions such as fear, greed, excitement, and frustration allows traders to better control their responses.

2. Controlling Fear and Greed:

Fear and greed are two powerful emotions that can lead to irrational decisions. Fear of losses may cause traders to exit winning trades too early, while greed may lead to holding losing positions for too long. Emotional management involves controlling these emotions to make rational and objective trading decisions.

3. Maintaining Emotional Discipline:

Emotional discipline is essential for sticking to a trading plan and following pre-defined rules. Traders should avoid making impulsive decisions based on emotions and instead rely on their trading strategies and risk management principles.

4. Dealing with Losses:

Emotional management helps traders cope with losses more effectively. Accepting losses as a normal part of trading and learning from them instead of dwelling on emotions like frustration or disappointment is crucial for improvement.

5. Avoiding Overtrading:

Emotional traders may fall into the trap of overtrading, taking excessive trades due to excitement or the desire to recover losses quickly. Emotional management helps traders avoid overtrading and maintain a disciplined approach to their trading activity.

6. Developing Patience:

Patience is a valuable virtue in Forex trading. Emotional management enables traders to wait for high-probability setups and not force trades out of impatience or fear of missing out.

7. Positive Self-Talk and Visualization:

Emotional management involves cultivating a positive mindset. Traders can use positive self-talk and visualization techniques to build confidence and reinforce their trading abilities.

8. Taking Breaks and Managing Stress:

Emotional management also includes recognizing when stress levels are high and taking breaks when needed. Managing stress helps traders maintain a clear and focused mind during trading.

9. Learning from Mistakes:

Emotional traders may tend to repeat mistakes or blame external factors for their losses. Emotional management encourages traders to take responsibility for their actions, learn from mistakes, and make necessary adjustments to improve their trading approach.

Emotional management is a vital skill for Forex traders to navigate the challenges of the market effectively. By understanding and controlling their emotions, traders can make rational and disciplined decisions, adhere to their trading plans, and maintain a positive trading mindset. Emotional management, combined with proper risk management and continuous learning, empowers traders to achieve consistency and success in the dynamic and competitive world of Forex trading. Developing emotional intelligence is an ongoing process that requires self-awareness, practice, and a commitment to personal growth.

7.3 Building a Resilient Mindset

Building a resilient mindset is essential for Forex traders to navigate the ups and downs of the market with confidence and adaptability. A resilient mindset enables traders to bounce back from setbacks, stay focused on their long-term goals, and maintain emotional discipline during trading. Here are some key strategies to build a resilient mindset in Forex trading:

1. **Embrace Learning and Growth:**

Resilient traders view trading as a continuous learning journey. They embrace new knowledge, seek feedback, and are open to improving their trading skills and strategies. A growth mindset allows traders to see challenges as opportunities for growth and development.

2. **Develop Emotional Intelligence:**

Understanding and managing emotions is crucial for resilience. Traders with emotional intelligence can recognize and control their emotions during trading, avoiding impulsive decisions driven by fear, greed, or frustration.

3. Focus on Process Over Outcomes:

Resilient traders focus on executing their trading plans effectively rather than fixating solely on the outcomes of individual trades. They understand that losses are part of the process and remain committed to following their strategies.

4. Cultivate Patience and Discipline:

Patience and discipline are key attributes of a resilient mindset. Traders with patience can wait for high-probability setups and avoid overtrading. Discipline allows them to stick to their trading rules and risk management principles.

5. Practice Mindfulness and Self-Reflection:

Mindfulness practices, such as meditation or deep breathing, can help traders stay present and focused during trading. Self-reflection allows traders to analyze their trading performance, identify strengths and weaknesses, and make necessary improvements.

6. Set Realistic Expectations:

Resilient traders set realistic expectations for their trading results. They understand that Forex trading is not a get-rich-quick scheme and that consistent profitability takes time, effort, and discipline.

7.   Adaptability and Flexibility:

The Forex market is dynamic, and resilient traders are adaptable and flexible in their approach. They can adjust their strategies and risk management techniques based on changing market conditions.

8.   Seek Support and Community:

Building a resilient mindset is easier with the support of like-minded traders or a trading community. Engaging with others can provide valuable insights, encouragement, and motivation.

9.   Focus on the Long Term:

Resilient traders maintain a long-term perspective and do not let short-term setbacks deter them. They understand that success in Forex trading is a journey of continuous improvement.

10. Embrace Failure as a Learning Opportunity:

Resilient traders view failure as an opportunity to learn and grow. They do not dwell on losses or mistakes but use them as valuable lessons to refine their trading approach.

Building a resilient mindset is crucial for Forex traders to navigate the challenges and uncertainties of the market successfully. By embracing learning and growth, developing emotional intelligence, practicing patience and discipline, and staying adaptable, traders can become more resilient in their trading journey. A resilient mindset allows traders to maintain focus, emotional discipline, and confidence, ultimately leading to improved trading performance and consistent long-term success in the dynamic and competitive world of Forex trading. Continuous practice, self-awareness, and commitment to personal growth are essential for building and sustaining a resilient mindset.

7.4 Managing Risk in Forex Trading

Managing risk is a fundamental and critical aspect of Forex trading. Effectively managing risk helps traders protect their capital, limit potential losses, and ensure their long-term survival in the market. Implementing sound risk management practices is essential for achieving consistent profitability and success. Here are some key strategies for managing risk in Forex trading:

1. Position Sizing:

Position sizing refers to determining the appropriate amount of capital to allocate to each trade. Traders should avoid risking a significant portion of their trading capital on a single trade. A common rule of thumb is to risk only a small percentage (e.g., 1% to 2%) of the total trading capital on each trade. Proper position sizing helps protect against significant drawdowns.

2. Setting Stop-Loss Orders:

Stop-loss orders are pre-defined price levels at which a trade will be automatically closed to limit potential losses. Placing stop-loss orders is crucial as it ensures that traders exit losing trades before losses become too large. Stop-loss orders should be set based on technical analysis, support and resistance levels, or other relevant factors.

3. Take-Profit Orders:

Take-profit orders are pre-defined price levels at which a trade will be automatically closed to secure profits. Having a target for profit-taking helps traders lock in gains when the market moves in their favor. Setting take-profit orders ensures that traders capitalize on favorable price movements.

4. Diversification:

Diversifying the trading portfolio across various currency pairs and other assets can help spread risk. Different currency pairs may have varying levels of volatility and correlation with each other, so diversification can reduce overall exposure to any single market.

5. Risk-Reward Ratio:

Assessing the risk-reward ratio before entering a trade is essential. A favorable risk-reward ratio means that the potential reward is higher than the potential risk. Traders should seek trades with a positive risk-reward ratio, where the potential profit outweighs the potential loss.

6. Avoiding Over-Leveraging:

Leverage amplifies both potential profits and losses in Forex trading. While leverage can magnify gains, it can also lead to substantial losses. Responsible traders avoid over-leveraging and use leverage prudently to manage risk.

7. Risk Management Tools:

Some trading platforms offer risk management tools, such as trailing stops or guaranteed stop-loss orders. These tools can help traders automate risk management and protect their positions in volatile market conditions.

8. Risk Tolerance and Trading Plan:

Traders should be aware of their risk tolerance level and develop a well-defined trading plan. The trading plan should outline risk management rules, trading strategies, and a clear set of rules for entering and exiting trades.

Managing risk in Forex trading is a crucial skill that separates successful traders from those who suffer significant losses. By implementing proper position sizing, setting stop-loss and take-profit orders, diversifying the trading portfolio, and using a favorable risk-reward ratio, traders can effectively manage risk and protect their capital. A disciplined and well-thought-out risk management approach is essential for achieving consistent profitability and long-term success in the dynamic and competitive world of Forex trading. Continuous practice, learning, and adaptation to changing market conditions are key to mastering risk management and becoming a successful Forex trader.

Chapter 8: Trading Psychology

Trading psychology is a critical aspect of successful Forex trading. It refers to the emotional and mental factors that influence a trader's decision-making process and behavior in the market. Mastering trading psychology is essential for maintaining emotional discipline, making rational decisions, and navigating the challenges of the market with confidence. In this chapter, we will explore key concepts and strategies related to trading psychology:

1. Emotions and Trading

Understanding Emotions: Traders must recognize and understand emotions that arise during trading, such as fear, greed, excitement, and frustration. Emotions can significantly impact decision-making and trading outcomes.

Controlling Fear and Greed: Fear and greed are two powerful emotions that can lead to impulsive decisions. Traders should develop emotional discipline to control these emotions and make rational trading choices.

Overcoming Loss Aversion: Loss aversion is the tendency to fear losses more than value gains. Resilient traders learn to accept losses as part of the trading process and avoid making irrational decisions to avoid losses.

2. Mental Discipline

Maintaining Emotional Discipline: Emotional discipline is crucial for adhering to a well-defined trading plan and executing trades based on strategy rather than emotions.

Staying Patient and Disciplined: Patience and discipline are essential virtues in Forex trading. Patient traders wait for high-probability setups and avoid overtrading, while disciplined traders stick to their trading rules and risk management principles.

3. Dealing with Losses

Accepting Losses: Losses are an inevitable part of trading. Emotionally resilient traders accept losses as a natural occurrence and focus on learning from them.

Avoiding Revenge Trading: Revenge trading, which involves trying to recover losses quickly, can lead to further losses. Emotionally disciplined traders avoid revenge trading and make decisions based on rational analysis.

4. Developing a Positive Mindset

Positive Self-Talk and Visualization: Traders can develop a positive mindset by using positive self-talk and visualization techniques. Believing in one's abilities and having confidence in trading strategies is essential for success.

Gratitude and Mindfulness: Practicing gratitude and mindfulness can help traders stay present and focused during trading, reducing the impact of distractions and emotions.

5. Building Resilience

Learning from Mistakes: Resilient traders view mistakes as learning opportunities and use them to improve their trading approach.

Setting Realistic Expectations: Setting realistic expectations for trading results helps traders stay grounded and committed to the long-term journey.

6. Continuous Learning and Adaptation

Continuous Learning: Forex markets are dynamic, and continuous learning is essential for staying updated with market trends and refining trading strategies.

Adapting to Market Conditions: Emotionally resilient traders remain adaptable and adjust their strategies to suit changing market conditions.

Trading psychology plays a pivotal role in a trader's success. By understanding and mastering emotions, maintaining emotional discipline, staying patient and disciplined, and cultivating a positive mindset, traders can enhance their decision-making process and achieve consistency in their trading performance. Building resilience, learning from mistakes, and embracing continuous learning and adaptation are keys to long-term success in the challenging and rewarding world of Forex trading. Traders who prioritize trading psychology alongside technical and fundamental analysis increase their chances of thriving in the dynamic and competitive Forex market. Continuous practice, self-awareness, and commitment to personal growth are essential for mastering trading psychology and becoming a successful Forex trader.

8.1 Overcoming Common Trading Mistakes

Overcoming common trading mistakes is essential for improving trading performance and achieving consistent profitability in Forex trading. Many traders fall into common pitfalls that can hinder their progress. By identifying and addressing these mistakes, traders can enhance their decision-making process and increase their chances of success. Here are some of the most common trading mistakes and strategies to overcome them:

1. Overtrading:

Overtrading occurs when traders execute too many trades, often driven by emotions like greed or the fear of missing out. Overtrading can lead to increased transaction costs and impulsive decisions. To overcome overtrading, traders should stick to their trading plan, wait for high-probability setups, and be patient in selecting trades that align with their strategies.

2. Revenge Trading:

Revenge trading happens when traders try to recover losses quickly by taking excessive risks or entering trades without proper analysis. To avoid revenge trading, traders should accept losses as part of the trading process, practice emotional discipline, and avoid making impulsive decisions based on emotions.

3. Ignoring Risk Management:

Neglecting risk management principles is a significant mistake. Proper risk management is crucial for protecting trading capital and limiting potential losses. Traders should use stop-loss orders, set appropriate position sizes, and adhere to their risk-reward ratios to manage risk effectively.

4. Chasing the Market:

Chasing the market occurs when traders enter trades too late, often at the peak of a trend or after significant price movements have already occurred. To avoid chasing the market, traders should wait for confirmation signals and not force trades based on fear of missing out on potential opportunities.

5. Lack of Trading Plan:

Trading without a well-defined trading plan is a recipe for failure. Traders should develop a comprehensive trading plan that includes entry and exit strategies, risk management rules, and guidelines for handling different market scenarios.

6. Emotional Trading:

Emotional trading, driven by fear, greed, or excitement, can lead to impulsive and irrational decisions. Traders should develop emotional discipline and learn to manage their emotions during trading. Using techniques such as mindfulness and self-awareness can help traders stay focused and make rational decisions.

7. Lack of Patience and Discipline:

Patience and discipline are vital for successful trading. Traders should wait for high-quality setups and avoid entering trades out of boredom or impatience. Sticking to trading rules and strategies is essential for maintaining discipline.

8. Neglecting Continuous Learning:

Forex markets are dynamic, and neglecting continuous learning can leave traders behind. To stay competitive, traders should invest in education, stay updated with market trends, and continuously improve their trading skills.

Overcoming common trading mistakes is crucial for becoming a successful Forex trader. By avoiding overtrading, revenge trading, and emotional decision-making, and by prioritizing risk management, discipline, and patience, traders can improve their trading performance. Developing a well-defined trading plan and continuous learning is key to overcoming mistakes and achieving consistent profitability in the dynamic and challenging world of Forex trading. Traders who remain disciplined, patient, and emotionally resilient are more likely to thrive in the competitive Forex market and build a successful and sustainable trading career.

8.2 Dealing with Losses

Dealing with losses is an inevitable aspect of Forex trading. Every trader, regardless of experience or skill level, will encounter losing trades at some point. How traders handle losses is critical for their long-term success and emotional well-being. Here are some effective strategies for dealing with losses in Forex trading:

1. Acceptance and Emotional Resilience:

Accepting losses as a natural part of trading is the first step to dealing with them effectively. Emotionally resilient traders understand that losses are unavoidable and do not let them affect their self-confidence or trading discipline.

2. Stay Calm and Avoid Emotional Trading:

Experiencing losses can trigger emotional reactions, such as frustration or fear. It is essential to stay calm and avoid making impulsive decisions driven by emotions. Emotional trading can lead to further losses and hinder a trader's ability to think rationally.

3. Analyze and Learn from Losses:

Instead of dwelling on losses, traders should analyze them to identify what went wrong. Learning from losses helps traders avoid making the same mistakes in the future and refine their trading strategies.

4. Stick to Your Trading Plan:

Having a well-defined trading plan is crucial for dealing with losses. Traders should stick to their plan and avoid deviating from it based on individual trade outcomes. Trusting the trading plan provides a framework for consistency and discipline.

5. Implement Effective Risk Management:

Proper risk management is essential for managing losses and protecting trading capital. Using stop-loss orders and position-sizing techniques can limit the impact of losses on a trader's account.

6. Avoid Chasing Losses (Revenge Trading):

Chasing losses or revenge trading is a common mistake that traders should avoid. Trying to quickly recover losses by taking excessive risks can lead to further losses. It is essential to remain disciplined and patient.

7. Take Breaks and Practice Self-Care:

Trading can be emotionally demanding, especially after experiencing losses. Taking breaks, practicing self-care, and engaging in activities outside of trading can help traders maintain a clear and focused mindset.

8. Focus on the Long Term:

Trading is a journey of continuous learning and improvement. Traders should focus on their long-term trading goals and not get discouraged by short-term losses.

9. Seek Support and Learning Opportunities:

Engaging with other traders or a trading community can provide valuable support and learning opportunities. Sharing experiences and insights with peers can help traders gain perspective and find new ways to improve their trading approach.

Dealing with losses is an integral part of Forex trading. Emotionally resilient traders accept losses as part of the trading process and use them as learning opportunities. By staying calm, adhering to their trading plan, implementing effective risk management, and maintaining a long-term perspective, traders can effectively deal with losses and maintain a disciplined and focused mindset. Developing emotional discipline and resilience is essential for navigating the challenges of trading and achieving consistent profitability in the dynamic and competitive Forex market. Continuous learning, self-awareness, and a commitment to improvement are key to becoming a successful and emotionally resilient Forex trader.

8.3 Staying Composed under Pressure

Staying composed under pressure is a crucial skill for Forex traders to make rational and well-thought-out decisions during challenging market conditions. The Forex market can be highly volatile and unpredictable, and maintaining composure is essential for successful trading. Here are some effective strategies to stay composed under pressure:

1. **Emphasize Emotional Discipline:**

Emotional discipline is the foundation of staying composed under pressure. Traders should recognize and manage their emotions effectively, especially during times of high volatility or significant market movements.

2. **Practice Mindfulness and Self-Awareness:**

Mindfulness techniques, such as deep breathing or meditation, can help traders stay present and focused during trading. Self-awareness allows traders to recognize when they are feeling stressed or anxious and take proactive steps to manage those emotions.

3. **Stick to Your Trading Plan:**

Having a well-defined trading plan provides a sense of direction and clarity during pressure situations. Traders should rely on their trading plan and avoid making impulsive decisions based on emotions or external market noise.

4. Use Effective Risk Management:

Implementing proper risk management techniques can alleviate some of the pressures of trading. Using stop-loss orders, setting appropriate position sizes, and managing leverage help protect trading capital and reduce the impact of potential losses.

5. Avoid Overtrading and Chasing the Market:

Overtrading and chasing the market are common mistakes made under pressure. Traders should avoid entering trades without proper analysis or taking excessive risks to recover losses quickly.

6. Focus on Process Over Outcomes:

Focusing on the trading process rather than being fixated on individual trade outcomes can help traders stay composed. Traders should concentrate on following their trading strategies and executing their plans with discipline.

7. Take Breaks and Manage Stress:

Stress can impair decision-making and increase emotional reactions. Taking short breaks during trading sessions and engaging in stress-relief activities outside of trading can help traders maintain a clear and composed mindset.

8. Limit Information Overload:

Being bombarded with too much information can increase stress and anxiety. Limit exposure to unnecessary market news and focus on relevant and actionable information.

9. Stay Humble and Learn from Mistakes:

Accepting that losses and mistakes are part of the trading journey can help traders stay humble and open to learning. Reflecting on past trades and learning from mistakes can lead to valuable insights and improvements.

10. Visualize Success and Stay Positive:

Positive visualization and self-affirmations can help traders build confidence and maintain composure during challenging market situations.

Staying composed under pressure is a vital skill for Forex traders to make rational decisions and navigate the market successfully. By emphasizing emotional discipline, practicing mindfulness, sticking to a trading plan, and using effective risk management techniques, traders can maintain composure and perform at their best even during stressful market conditions. Continuous self-awareness, learning, and a commitment to personal growth are key to developing the ability to stay composed and thrive in the dynamic and competitive world of Forex trading.

8.4 The Trader's Mindset for Success

The trader's mindset is a crucial factor in achieving success in Forex trading. A strong and disciplined mindset sets successful traders apart from the rest. Developing the right mindset involves adopting specific attitudes and approaches that promote consistent profitability and long-term success. Here are essential components of the trader's mindset for success:

1. Positive Attitude: A positive attitude is the foundation of a successful trader's mindset. Positive thinkers are more likely to stay motivated, focused, and resilient during challenging market conditions. They believe in their abilities and have confidence in their trading strategies.
2. Emotional Discipline: Emotional discipline is vital for making rational and objective trading decisions. Successful traders maintain control over their emotions, avoid impulsive actions, and stick to their trading plan even during periods of market turbulence.Adaptability: Forex markets are constantly changing, and successful traders are adaptable. They have the ability to adjust their strategies and approaches to suit different market conditions and stay ahead of the curve.
3. Patience and Discipline: Patience and discipline go hand in hand in Forex trading. Patient traders wait for high-probability trade setups

and avoid rushing into trades out of impatience. Discipline helps traders stick to their trading rules and risk management principles.

4. Continuous Learning: Successful traders are committed to continuous learning and self-improvement. They stay updated with market trends, study market analysis, and learn from both successes and failures to refine their trading strategies.

5. Risk Management Focus: Risk management is at the core of the trader's mindset for success. Effective risk management techniques protect capital and limit potential losses, ensuring traders' long-term survival in the market.

6. Realistic Expectations: Successful traders have realistic expectations about their trading results. They understand that consistent profitability takes time and effort and do not fall for get-rich-quick schemes.

7. Self-Reflection: Reflecting on past trades and performance helps traders identify strengths, weaknesses, and areas for improvement. Self-reflection allows traders to grow and evolve as traders.

8. Resilience: Resilient traders bounce back from losses and setbacks, remaining focused on their long-term goals. They view challenges as opportunities for growth and learning.

9. Focus on Process Over Outcomes: Successful traders focus on executing their trading strategies effectively, rather than obsessing over individual trade outcomes. They understand that following a solid trading plan leads to success in the long run.

10. Confidence in Decision-Making: Confidence in decision-making comes from a deep understanding of the markets and strategies. Successful traders trust their analysis and stick to their convictions.

The trader's mindset for success encompasses positive attitudes, emotional discipline, adaptability, patience, continuous learning, and a strong focus on risk management. Developing and maintaining the right mindset is essential for achieving consistent profitability and long-term success in the competitive and dynamic world of Forex trading. Traders who cultivate the trader's mindset build the resilience, discipline, and confidence necessary to navigate the challenges of trading and thrive in the ever-changing Forex market. Continuous practice, self-awareness, and a commitment to personal growth are key to nurturing the trader's mindset and becoming a successful Forex trader.

Chapter 9: Developing a Winning Trading Plan

A winning trading plan is a roadmap that guides Forex traders to make well-informed and strategic decisions. It serves as a blueprint for achieving consistent profitability and long-term success in the market. A comprehensive trading plan includes specific trading strategies, risk management guidelines, and rules for trade execution. In this chapter, we will explore the essential components of a winning trading plan:

1. Setting Clear Goals

- Defining Trading Objectives: Traders should set clear and achievable trading objectives, such as a target return on investment, monthly profit goals, or annual growth targets.
- Timeframe and Trading Style: Determining the preferred trading timeframe (e.g., day trading, swing trading, or position trading) and trading style helps shape the overall trading plan.

2. Market Analysis and Strategy

- Technical Analysis: Describe the technical analysis tools and indicators to be used for identifying entry and exit points. This may include moving averages, support and resistance levels, and chart patterns.
- Fundamental Analysis: Detail the fundamental factors to be considered in the trading plan, such as economic indicators, geopolitical events, and central bank policies.

- Entry and Exit Rules: Define the criteria for entering and exiting trades based on the chosen technical and fundamental analysis methods.
- Risk-Reward Ratio: Specify the minimum risk-reward ratio for each trade to ensure that potential profits outweigh potential losses.

3. Risk Management

- Position Sizing: Describe the position sizing technique to determine the appropriate amount of capital to allocate to each trade, taking into account risk tolerance and account size.
- Stop-Loss and Take-Profit Orders: Detail how stop-loss and take-profit orders will be set to protect capital and secure profits.
- Maximum Daily or Weekly Loss Limit: Establish a maximum allowable loss per trading day or week to prevent excessive drawdowns.
- Leverage Usage: Define the maximum leverage to be used in trades to control risk exposure.

4. Trading Psychology and Discipline

- Emotional Management: Describe strategies for managing emotions and staying disciplined during trading, including mindfulness and self-awareness techniques.
- Learning from Mistakes: Include a plan for self-reflection and learning from past trades and mistakes.

- Avoiding Overtrading and Revenge Trading: Outline steps to prevent overtrading and revenge trading, such as taking breaks during periods of stress.

5. Review and Evaluation

- Performance Analysis: Specify how trading performance will be evaluated, including tracking key performance metrics, such as win rate and profit factor.
- Adjustment and Improvement: Describe how the trading plan will be reviewed regularly, and adjustments will be made based on changing market conditions and trading performance.

A winning trading plan is a critical tool for Forex traders to achieve consistent profitability and long-term success. By setting clear goals, defining market analysis strategies, implementing effective risk management, and maintaining emotional discipline, traders can develop a winning trading plan that suits their trading style and objectives. Continuous evaluation and improvement of the trading plan based on performance analysis are essential for staying adaptive and competitive in the dynamic Forex market. Traders who follow a well-structured trading plan are better equipped to navigate the challenges of trading and build a successful and sustainable trading career.

9.1 Setting Realistic Goals

Setting realistic goals is a fundamental aspect of achieving success in Forex trading. Realistic goals provide traders with clear direction, motivation, and a sense of accomplishment as they work towards achieving their objectives. Unrealistic goals can lead to frustration, impulsive decisions, and increased risk-taking. Here are some strategies for setting realistic goals in Forex trading:

- Be Specific and Measurable: Define your trading goals in specific and measurable terms. Instead of a vague goal like "making a lot of money," set specific targets, such as a certain percentage of return on investment or a monthly profit goal.
- Consider Your Trading Style: Your trading style and time commitment play a crucial role in setting realistic goals. Day traders, swing traders, and position traders may have different profit expectations and risk tolerance levels.
- Assess Your Trading Capital: Consider the amount of trading capital you have available. Realistic goals should align with your account size and risk management principles.
- Understand Market Realities: Forex trading involves inherent risks, and markets can be unpredictable. Set goals based on historical market performance and avoid expecting consistent profits in every trade.
- Set Long-Term and Short-Term Goals: Divide your goals into long-term and short-term objectives. Long-term goals may focus on annual or multi-year targets, while short-term goals can be weekly or monthly targets.
- Gradual Growth Approach: Aim for gradual growth in your trading performance. Avoid setting overly ambitious targets that require high-risk strategies.

- Focus on the Process: Instead of solely focusing on the outcome, emphasize the process of executing your trading plan effectively. Concentrate on following your strategies and adhering to risk management principles.
- Learn from Past Performance: Analyze your past trading performance to understand your strengths and weaknesses. Use this information to set realistic goals that take into account your historical performance.
- Be Flexible and Adaptive: Markets change, and setting realistic goals requires flexibility. Be prepared to adjust your goals based on changing market conditions and performance evaluation.
- Celebrate Achievements: Acknowledge and celebrate your achievements, even if they are small steps towards your long-term goals. Recognizing progress boosts motivation and confidence.

Setting realistic goals is essential for Forex traders to maintain a disciplined and focused approach to their trading journey. By being specific and measurable, considering trading style and capital, understanding market realities, and focusing on both short-term and long-term objectives, traders can develop achievable and motivating goals. Emphasizing the process over outcomes and learning from past performance supports continuous improvement and growth. Being flexible and celebrating achievements along the way fosters a positive and determined mindset. Setting realistic goals not only increases the likelihood of success but also contributes to a sustainable and fulfilling trading experience in the dynamic and challenging world of Forex trading.

9.2 Backtesting Strategies

Backtesting strategies are a crucial step in the development and evaluation of trading systems in Forex. Backtesting involves testing a trading strategy using historical market data to assess its performance and profitability. It helps traders identify the strengths and weaknesses of a strategy and whether it is likely to be successful in real-time trading. Here are the key steps and considerations for backtesting strategies in Forex:

1. **Define the Trading Strategy:**

Clearly outline the rules and parameters of the trading strategy to be tested. This includes entry and exit criteria, stop-loss and take-profit levels, and any other relevant rules.

2. **Gather Historical Market Data:**

Obtain reliable and accurate historical price data for the currency pairs and timeframes relevant to the strategy being tested. The data should include price quotes, volume, and other necessary information.

3. **Choose Backtesting Software:**

Select a backtesting software or platform that suits your needs. There are various software options available, both free and paid, that can facilitate the process of backtesting.

4. Set Up the Backtest:

Input the trading strategy rules and parameters into the backtesting software. Adjust any settings or parameters as needed to accurately represent the strategy.

5. Run the Backtest:

Execute the backtest using the historical market data. The software will apply the trading strategy to past price data to simulate trading results.

6. Analyze the Results:

Review and analyze the backtesting results. Assess metrics such as total profit or loss, average profit or loss per trade, win rate, drawdown, and risk-reward ratio.

7. Consider Slippage and Spread:

Take into account slippage (the difference between the intended price and the actual executed price) and spread (the difference between the bid and ask price) during the backtest to better reflect real-world trading conditions.

8. Validate and Optimize the Strategy:

Evaluate the performance of the strategy and identify any potential flaws or areas for improvement. If necessary, refine the strategy and re-run the backtest to optimize its parameters.

9. Be Cautious of Overfitting:

Avoid overfitting the strategy to historical data. Overfitting occurs when a strategy is excessively tailored to historical data, resulting in good backtesting performance but poor real-time performance.

10. Use Out-of-Sample Testing:

For validation, use out-of-sample testing by applying the optimized strategy to a separate set of historical data not used in the initial backtest. This helps assess the strategy's robustness.

Backtesting strategies are a critical step in the development and evaluation of trading systems in Forex. It allows traders to assess the performance and viability of a strategy using historical market data. By carefully defining the strategy, selecting appropriate backtesting software, analyzing the results, and avoiding overfitting, traders can gain valuable insights into the potential effectiveness of their trading strategies. However, it is essential to remember that past performance does not guarantee future results, and forward testing in a demo or live trading environment is necessary to validate the strategy's performance in real-time market conditions.

9.3 Optimizing Trading Plans

Optimizing trading plans is a continuous process of refining and improving trading strategies and risk management techniques to enhance overall performance and profitability. Successful traders regularly review and adjust their trading plans to adapt to changing market conditions and incorporate valuable insights gained from experience. Here are key strategies for optimizing trading plans:

1. **Regular Performance Evaluation:**

Regularly evaluate the performance of the trading plan by analyzing trading results, including profitability, win rate, drawdowns, and risk-reward ratio. This evaluation helps identify strengths and weaknesses in the plan.

2. **Identify Areas for Improvement:**

Based on the performance evaluation, pinpoint areas of the trading plan that require improvement. This may include refining entry and exit strategies, adjusting risk management rules, or incorporating new analysis techniques.

3. **Backtesting and Forward Testing:**

Perform backtesting and forward testing on the optimized elements of the trading plan. Backtesting helps assess historical performance, while forward testing allows traders to validate the changes in a real-time market environment.

4.   Risk Management Enhancements:

Strengthen risk management techniques to protect capital and limit potential losses. This may involve adjusting position sizing, setting tighter stop-loss orders, or implementing trailing stops.

5.   Embrace Flexibility:

Stay flexible and open to adapting the trading plan as market conditions change. Markets are dynamic, and a rigid trading plan may become ineffective over time.

6.   Learn from Mistakes:

Analyze past mistakes and losing trades to learn from them. Incorporate the lessons learned into the trading plan to avoid repeating the same errors.

7.   Avoid Over-Optimization:

Be cautious of over-optimization, also known as curve-fitting, where the trading plan is excessively tailored to historical data but performs poorly in real-time trading. Focus on robust strategies that work across different market conditions.

8. Set Realistic Goals:

Set achievable and realistic trading goals based on historical performance and risk tolerance. Unrealistic goals can lead to frustration and impulsive decision-making.

9. Review External Factors:

Consider external factors that may impact the trading plan, such as economic events, geopolitical developments, or central bank policies. Stay informed about market news and incorporate relevant information into the plan.

10. Keep a Trading Journal:

Maintain a trading journal to record trades, decisions, and emotions. Reviewing the journal helps gain insights into trading behavior and identify areas for improvement.

11. Seek Feedback and Guidance:

Seek feedback from experienced traders or trading communities. Engaging with peers provides valuable perspectives and helps validate or refine the optimization process.

Optimizing trading plans is an ongoing process that involves evaluating performance, identifying areas for improvement, and adapting to changing market conditions. By regularly reviewing and adjusting the trading plan, incorporating risk management enhancements, and avoiding over-optimization, traders can continuously improve their trading strategies and increase their chances of consistent profitability. Staying flexible, setting realistic goals, and learning from mistakes are key components of a successful optimization process. Traders who embrace a growth mindset and prioritize continuous improvement are more likely to thrive in the dynamic and competitive world of Forex trading.

9.4 Keeping a Trading Journal

Keeping a trading journal is an essential practice for Forex traders to record and analyze their trading activities. It serves as a valuable tool for self-improvement, learning from past trades, and maintaining discipline in the trading process. Here are the key reasons why traders should keep a trading journal:

1. **Trade Records:**

A trading journal helps traders maintain a detailed record of their trades, including entry and exit points, trade size, stop-loss and take-profit levels, and the reasoning behind each trade.

2. Performance Analysis:

Traders can use the trading journal to analyze their trading performance over time. It allows them to review their profit and loss, win rate, risk-reward ratios, and other key performance metrics.

3. Identifying Strengths and Weaknesses:

By analyzing past trades, traders can identify their strengths and weaknesses. They can capitalize on their strengths and work on improving their weaknesses.

4. Learning from Mistakes:

Recording losing trades and mistakes in the trading journal enables traders to learn from their errors. It helps them avoid repeating the same mistakes and refine their trading strategies.

5. Emotional Discipline:

Keeping track of emotions during trading is essential for emotional discipline. Traders can note their emotional state when entering and exiting trades, helping them make more rational decisions.

6. **Trade Management:**

A trading journal helps traders review how well they adhered to their trading plan and risk management rules during each trade.

7. **Psychological Insights:**

Traders can use the journal to gain insights into their psychological responses to winning and losing trades. It helps them work on maintaining a balanced emotional state during trading.

8. **Evaluation of Strategies:**

Traders can assess the performance of different trading strategies by comparing their results in the trading journal.

9. **Goal Tracking:**

Traders can track progress toward their trading goals in the journal. This enables them to stay motivated and focused on achieving their objectives.

10. **Decision-Making Improvement:**

Through self-reflection, traders can improve their decision-making process by understanding the reasoning behind each trade.

How to Keep a Trading Journal:

1. Record every trade in a consistent and organized format, either manually or using electronic tools or software.
2. Include essential details for each trade, such as the currency pair, entry and exit points, trade size, stop-loss, take-profit levels, and trade duration.
3. Document the market conditions and factors that influenced the trade.
4. Analyze each trade, noting the outcome and any lessons learned.
5. Regularly review and analyze the journal to identify patterns and areas for improvement.
6. Use the journal as a tool for self-reflection and personal growth as a trader.

Keeping a trading journal is a valuable practice that empowers Forex traders to evaluate their performance, identify areas for improvement, and refine their strategies. It aids in maintaining discipline, emotional control, and a focused mindset. By consistently recording and analyzing trades, traders can learn from their experiences, make better decisions, and progress toward becoming more successful and consistent traders in the dynamic and competitive Forex market.

Chapter 10: Achieving Consistent Profits and Financial Freedom

Achieving consistent profits and financial freedom in Forex trading requires a combination of discipline, skill, and a well-defined approach. In this chapter, we will explore the key principles and strategies that can help traders reach their goal of consistent profitability and financial independence:

1. Mastering Emotional Discipline:

Emotional discipline is the foundation of successful trading. Traders must learn to manage emotions like fear and greed, avoid impulsive decisions, and stick to their trading plans even during challenging market conditions.

2. Implementing Effective Risk Management:

Proper risk management is essential for preserving trading capital and limiting losses. Traders should use appropriate position sizing, set stop-loss orders, and avoid over-leveraging.

3. Developing a Winning Trading Plan:

A well-structured trading plan, based on sound analysis and risk management, provides a roadmap for consistent profitability. Traders should backtest and optimize their strategies to enhance performance.

4. Continuous Learning and Improvement:

Forex markets are dynamic, and continuous learning is vital for staying competitive. Traders should invest in education, attend webinars, and read market analyses to stay updated with the latest trends and techniques.

5. Adapting to Changing Market Conditions:

Successful traders are adaptable and adjust their strategies to suit different market environments. Staying flexible and open to change ensures relevance and effectiveness.

6. Avoiding Overtrading and Chasing Losses:

Overtrading and chasing losses are common pitfalls that can lead to significant losses. Traders should stay patient, wait for high-probability setups, and avoid letting emotions dictate their trading decisions.

7. Trading with Realistic Expectations:

Forex trading is not a get-rich-quick scheme. Traders should set realistic profit goals and avoid unrealistic expectations that can lead to frustration and impulsive behavior.

8. Building a Diversified Portfolio:

Diversifying trading strategies and currency pairs can spread risk and increase the chances of consistent profits. A well-diversified portfolio can weather market fluctuations more effectively.

9. Maintaining Financial Discipline:

Financial discipline is essential outside of trading as well. Traders should manage personal finances responsibly and avoid taking excessive risks in their overall financial life.

10. Balancing Trading with Life:

Maintaining a healthy work-life balance is crucial for sustained success. Traders should avoid becoming overly obsessed with trading and take time for relaxation, hobbies, and relationships.

11. Patience and Perseverance:

Consistent profitability takes time and effort. Traders should remain patient and persevere through challenges and setbacks. Trusting the process and staying committed is key to achieving financial freedom.

Achieving consistent profits and financial freedom in Forex trading requires a combination of technical skills, emotional discipline, and a well-defined trading plan. By mastering risk management, continuously learning and adapting, and avoiding common trading mistakes, traders can increase their chances of success. Setting realistic goals, balancing trading with life, and maintaining financial discipline contribute to long-term financial independence. Consistency, perseverance, and a growth mindset are essential for traders to thrive in the dynamic and competitive world of Forex trading. With dedication and commitment to continuous improvement, traders can realize their dreams of achieving consistent profits and attaining financial freedom through successful Forex trading.

10.1 Adapting to Changing Market Conditions

Adapting to changing market conditions is a critical skill for Forex traders to remain successful and profitable in the dynamic and ever-evolving financial markets. Market conditions can vary from trending to ranging, high volatility to low volatility, and bullish to bearish sentiments. To navigate these shifts effectively, traders need to be flexible and adjust their trading strategies accordingly. Here are key strategies for adapting to changing market conditions:

1. **Stay Informed and Updated:**

Traders should constantly monitor market news, economic events, and geopolitical developments that may impact currency pairs. Staying informed about market fundamentals helps anticipate potential shifts in market sentiment.

2. **Understand Different Market Environments:**

Be familiar with different market environments, such as trending, ranging, or consolidating markets. Each environment requires different trading strategies, and recognizing them can help traders adjust their approach accordingly.

3. Use Multiple Timeframes:

Analyze price action and trends on multiple timeframes. This helps in gaining a comprehensive view of the market and identifying trends or patterns that may not be evident in a single timeframe.

4. Be Adaptable in Trading Strategies:

A trading plan should allow for flexibility and multiple strategies. When market conditions change, traders can switch to strategies that align better with the current environment.

5. Monitor Volatility:

Volatility affects the frequency and magnitude of price movements. During high volatility, traders may consider adjusting stop-loss levels and position sizes to account for larger price swings.

6. Adjust Risk Management:

Changing market conditions may require adjustments to risk management techniques. In highly volatile markets, traders may choose wider stop-loss levels, and in low volatility, they might opt for tighter stop-losses.

7. Be Patient in Ranging Markets:

During ranging markets, where prices move within a specific range, traders may need to exercise patience and avoid forcing trades. Waiting for clear breakouts or bounces from support and resistance levels can be more effective.

8. Trade Different Currency Pairs:

If certain currency pairs are not performing well in current market conditions, explore opportunities in other pairs that may be better suited to the prevailing environment.

9. Monitor Technical Indicators:

Technical indicators can provide valuable insights into market conditions. Adapt the use of technical indicators to align with the current price action and trends.

10. Learn from Past Adaptations:

Review past instances when you adapted to changing market conditions. Analyze the outcomes to identify successful adjustments and incorporate them into future trading plans.

11. Stay Disciplined:

While adapting to changing conditions, it's crucial to maintain discipline and avoid making impulsive decisions. Stick to your trading plan and only implement changes that align with your overall strategy.

Adapting to changing market conditions is a necessary skill for Forex traders to remain profitable and successful in the long run. By staying informed, understanding different market environments, using multiple timeframes, and adjusting strategies and risk management techniques, traders can effectively navigate evolving market dynamics. Embracing adaptability, combined with a disciplined approach to trading, allows traders to capitalize on opportunities and achieve consistent profitability in the dynamic and competitive Forex market. Continuous learning, self-awareness, and a willingness to adjust to market changes are key factors in mastering the art of adapting to changing market conditions.

10.2 Analyzing and Improving Trading Performance

Analyzing and improving trading performance is a crucial process for Forex traders to enhance their skills, increase profitability, and achieve consistent success in the market. By carefully evaluating past trades and identifying areas for improvement, traders can refine their strategies and make better-informed decisions. Here are the key steps for analyzing and improving trading performance:

1. **Maintain a Detailed Trading Journal:**

Keep a comprehensive trading journal that records all trades, including entry and exit points, trade size, stop-loss, take-profit levels, trade duration, and the reasoning behind each trade. Include notes on emotions and observations during the trade.

2. **Review Trading Performance Regularly:**

Regularly review and analyze your trading performance. Assess key performance metrics, such as total profit or loss, win rate, risk-reward ratio, and drawdown. This evaluation provides insights into your trading strengths and weaknesses.

3. **Identify Patterns and Mistakes:**

Analyze the trading journal to identify recurring patterns in successful trades and mistakes made in losing trades. Recognize common errors and focus on eliminating them from future trades.

4. **Backtesting and Forward Testing:**

Backtest your trading strategies using historical data to evaluate their past performance. Forward test the optimized strategies in a demo or live trading environment to validate their effectiveness in real-time market conditions.

5. Use Performance Analytics Tools:

Leverage trading platforms and performance analytics tools to assess your trading data and gain insights into your trading behavior.

6. Seek Feedback and Mentoring:

Seek feedback from experienced traders or consider joining trading communities where you can discuss your performance and receive valuable insights and guidance.

7. Set Realistic Goals for Improvement:

Set specific and achievable goals for improving your trading performance. This might include increasing the win rate, improving risk-reward ratios, or reducing emotional decision-making.

8. Focus on Risk Management:

Review your risk management techniques and adjust them as needed to protect capital and limit losses. Ensure that position sizing, stop-loss levels, and risk exposure align with your risk tolerance.

9. Continuously Learn and Update Strategies:

Stay updated with market trends, attend webinars, read educational resources, and continuously learn from experienced traders. Update your trading strategies based on new insights and market developments.

10. Practice Patience and Discipline:

Practice patience and discipline in following your trading plan. Avoid impulsive decisions and stick to your strategies even during challenging market conditions.

11. Evaluate the Impact of Market Conditions:

Consider the impact of different market conditions on your trading performance. Assess your ability to adapt to various market environments and make necessary adjustments.

12. Use Positive Reinforcement:

Celebrate your successes and achievements in trading to reinforce positive behavior and motivation.

Analyzing and improving trading performance is an ongoing process that involves meticulous record-keeping, self-reflection, and a commitment to learning and growth. By maintaining a detailed trading journal, reviewing performance regularly, identifying patterns and mistakes, backtesting and forward-testing strategies, and seeking feedback and mentoring, traders can continuously enhance their trading skills and increase profitability. Emphasizing risk management, setting realistic improvement goals, and maintaining discipline are key components of successful performance analysis and improvement. With dedication and a willingness to learn from both successes and setbacks, traders can achieve consistent success and grow as traders in the competitive world of Forex trading.

10.3 Balancing Risk and Reward

Balancing risk and reward is a crucial aspect of successful Forex trading. It involves finding a harmonious relationship between the potential gains from trade and the associated risks. Effective risk-reward management ensures that the potential reward justifies the level of risk taken, helping traders maintain consistent profitability and protect their trading capital. Here are key strategies for balancing risk and reward in Forex trading:

1. **Define Risk Tolerance:**

Understand your risk tolerance level based on your financial situation, trading experience, and emotional temperament. This will help you determine the maximum acceptable risk per trade.

2. **Use Appropriate Position Sizing:**

Adopt position sizing techniques that align with your risk tolerance and trading strategy. Avoid risking a significant portion of your capital on a single trade, as this can lead to substantial losses.

3.   Set Stop-Loss Orders:

Always use stop-loss orders to limit potential losses on each trade. Set stop-loss levels based on technical analysis, support and resistance levels, or other relevant criteria.

4.   Calculate Risk-Reward Ratio:

Assess the potential risk-reward ratio before entering a trade. Aim for a favorable risk-reward ratio, where the potential reward is significantly greater than the potential risk.

5.   Aim for Positive Expectancy:

Strive for a trading strategy with a positive expectancy, meaning that, on average, your winning trades yield more profit than your losing trades incur losses.

6.   Avoid Overtrading:

Overtrading can increase the overall risk exposure. Focus on high-probability trade setups and avoid taking excessive trades out of impatience or excitement.

7.   Use Trailing Stops:

Implement trailing stops to lock in profits as a trade moves in your favor. This allows you to ride winning trades while protecting against potential reversals.

8. Diversify Trading Strategies:

Utilize a diversified portfolio of trading strategies. This can help spread risk and adapt to different market conditions.

9. Be Realistic in Profit Targets:

Set realistic profit targets that consider the prevailing market conditions and the potential price movements. Avoid being overly optimistic about profit expectations.

10. Stay Disciplined:

Maintain discipline in adhering to your risk management rules and trading plan. Avoid deviating from your strategies due to emotional impulses.

11. Assess Risk-Adjusted Returns:

Evaluate the risk-adjusted returns of your trading performance, considering both the gains and the risks taken. This gives a more comprehensive view of overall profitability.

12. Continuously Monitor and Adjust:

Constantly monitor your trading performance and risk-reward balance. Be willing to adjust your strategies if needed to achieve a better balance.

Balancing risk and reward is essential for long-term success in Forex trading. By defining risk tolerance, using appropriate position sizing and stop-loss orders, calculating risk-reward ratios, and aiming for positive expectancy, traders can effectively manage risk while pursuing profitable opportunities. Staying disciplined, avoiding overtrading, and continuously monitoring and adjusting your approach contribute to maintaining a healthy risk-reward balance. Striking the right balance between risk and reward is a key skill that allows traders to thrive in the dynamic and competitive Forex market while preserving their trading capital and achieving consistent profitability.

10.4 Achieving Financial Freedom through Forex Trading

Achieving financial freedom through Forex trading is a goal that many traders aspire to. Forex trading offers the potential for substantial profits and the freedom to be one's own boss, but it also comes with inherent risks. To attain financial freedom through Forex trading, traders must adopt a disciplined and strategic approach. Here are key strategies to work toward financial freedom:

1. Education and Skill Development:

Invest in education and skill development to become a knowledgeable and skilled Forex trader. Understanding market dynamics, technical and fundamental analysis, and risk management is crucial for consistent profitability.

2.   Start with Sufficient Capital:

Begin trading with sufficient capital to withstand initial losses and prevent overtrading. Adequate capital provides the flexibility to take advantage of profitable opportunities without excessive risk.

3.   Set Realistic Goals:

Set clear and achievable financial goals. Aim for steady and sustainable growth rather than expecting overnight riches. Realistic goals prevent unrealistic expectations and emotional decision-making.

4.   Develop a Solid Trading Plan:

Create a comprehensive trading plan that outlines your strategies, risk management rules, and trading objectives. Stick to the plan and avoid impulsive trading.

5.   Practice Patience and Discipline:

Patience and discipline are crucial virtues in Forex trading. Avoid chasing quick profits and stay focused on executing your trading plan with discipline.

6. Emphasize Risk Management:

Implement effective risk management techniques, such as setting stop-loss orders and position sizing, to protect your capital and limit potential losses.

7. Diversify Your Portfolio:

Diversify your trading portfolio by trading multiple currency pairs and using various trading strategies. Diversification can spread risk and increase the potential for consistent profits.

8. Manage Emotions:

Mastering emotional control is vital for successful trading. Avoid making decisions based on fear or greed, and learn to stay calm and composed during both winning and losing trades.

9. Learn from Mistakes:

View losses and mistakes as learning opportunities. Analyze your trades to identify areas for improvement and avoid repeating the same errors.

10. Focus on Long-Term Growth:

Maintain a long-term perspective and aim for steady growth over time. Avoid excessive risk-taking for quick gains, as it can lead to significant losses.

11. Continuously Learn and Adapt:

Stay updated with market trends and adapt to changing market conditions. Continuous learning and improvement are essential for staying competitive.

12. Build Multiple Streams of Income:

Consider diversifying your sources of income beyond Forex trading. Building multiple streams of income can provide financial stability and support your trading efforts.

Achieving financial freedom through Forex trading requires dedication, education, and discipline. By setting realistic goals, developing a solid trading plan, emphasizing risk management, and continuously learning and adapting, traders can work towards financial independence. Forex trading can offer significant opportunities, but it also involves inherent risks. A patient and disciplined approach, combined with a commitment to personal growth and improvement, can lead to a successful and fulfilling journey toward financial freedom through Forex trading.

Conclusion

In conclusion, "Forex Trading: Decoding the Secrets of the Forex Market for Consistent Profits, Financial Freedom, and Success with Expert Navigation Techniques" is a comprehensive guide that unlocks the mysteries of Forex trading and empowers traders to embark on a journey toward financial independence and success. Throughout this book, we have explored the fundamental principles, strategies, and techniques necessary for achieving consistent profitability in the dynamic and competitive world of Forex.

The book began by providing a thorough understanding of the Forex market, its history, evolution, and major participants. We delved into the significance of expert navigation techniques and their role in guiding traders toward their financial goals.

Chapter by chapter, we covered the basics of Forex trading, decoding the market with fundamental and technical analysis, and harnessing sentiment and Intermarket analysis to make informed decisions. We discussed the crucial aspects of building a strong foundation, setting up a trading account, and implementing effective risk management strategies to protect capital.

The book further explored the art of developing a well-structured trading plan, maintaining discipline in the face of market pressures, and employing a range of trading strategies, including day trading, swing trading, carry trading and breakout trading.

Chart patterns, technical indicators, Fibonacci retracements, Elliott Wave theory, price action trading, and trading divergences were unveiled as advanced techniques to sharpen traders' analytical skills and boost their trading edge.

Recognizing the psychological aspects of trading, we delved into the trader's mindset for success, emotional management, and building a resilient mentality to navigate the ups and downs of the market.

Throughout the chapters, we emphasized the significance of analyzing and improving trading performance, achieving a balanced risk-reward ratio, and adapting to changing market conditions. All these facets contribute to the ultimate goal of achieving financial freedom through Forex trading.

Aspiring traders and seasoned professionals alike can draw upon the knowledge, wisdom, and practical guidance provided in this book. Emphasizing the importance of continuous learning, discipline, and a patient approach, we instilled the belief that with dedication and commitment to self-improvement, financial freedom through Forex trading is attainable.

May this book serve as a beacon of knowledge, illuminating the path toward consistent profits, financial freedom, and success in the vast and thrilling landscape of Forex trading. Remember, the secrets of the Forex market are not elusive; they are within reach, waiting to be unlocked by those who dare to decode them. Happy trading!

www.ingramcontent.com/pod-product-compliance
Lightning Source LLC
Chambersburg PA
CBHW082210290526

45794CB00009B/3496